Time Management is Life Management

Rinkal Sharma
Amit Sharma

DIAMOND BOOKS
www.diamondbook.in

All rights are reserved. No part of this publication may be reproduced, stored in a retrieval system or transmitted in any form or by any means, electronic, mechanical, photocopying, recording or otherwise, without the prior permission of the copyright holder.

© Publisher

Publisher	:	**Diamond Pocket Books (P) Ltd.**
		X-30, Okhla Industrial Area, Phase-II
		New Delhi-110020
Phone	:	011- 40712200
E-mail	:	sales@dpb.in
Website	:	www.diamondbook.in

Time Management is Life Management
Authors : *Rinkal Sharma & Amit Sharma*

About the Authors

Rinkal Sharma

An established author of many wonderful books in the field of language & its legacy, literatures & kids education in the form of short stories and poems, is also a social activist and actively involved in the field of theatre, TV & web-series by her skilled writing work. Her popular books are- Hindi ke Nau Sarathi, Urdu ke Nau Maharathi, Learn French through English, Learn French through Hindi, Masti ki Pathshala, Dil to Bachcha hai, Kaise Banega Aatmnirbhar Bharat. She is Secretary, Human Rights Council of India. She is editorial board member of Magazines Prabal Prahari, Anti-Crime, Ganga Mahima, Hindi Sahitya Sansthika, Ambe Bharti.

Mail-id - rinkalsharma@gmail.com

Amit Sharma

Professionally, Amit is working in leadership position with Big4 Consulting Firm and have niche experience of working closely in Government Advisory on many marquee projects. He also writes article regularly to newspaper World Mirror. He is passionate about sharing the ideas in this books and regularly speaks at conventions and training events. Unsurprising to those who know him, Amit believes that his single greatest achievement is the life he has built with his wife Rinkal and their son, Arjun Pandit.

Acknowledgement

Any accomplishment requires the efforts of many people and this work is not different. I thank my son Arjun Pandit and especially my wife Rinkal Sharma, whose patience and support was instrumental in accomplishing this task. They both are the rich sources of energy behind my every accomplishment, not only this book. Also, blessings of our parents is also a source behind everything we achieve.

Many examples, stories, anecdotes are the result of a collection from various sources such as newspapers, magazines, other speakers, and seminar participants, over the last two decades. Unfortunately, the sources were not always noted or available; hence, it became impractical to provide an accurate acknowledgement. Regardless of the sources, I wish to express my gratitude to all those who may have contributed in the domain of Time Management and have been inspirational and guiding force considering Time Management and its practices are a universal concept. I must admit, all such people touched me with their learnings and experiences. I only attempted to walk few steps on this journey.

I voraciously read many books, business magazines, blogs, research papers whose learning have touched me significantly over a period. In my writing, genius of all those authors have reflection as they have touched my soul with their exceptional work. Without these writings and references from these thought leaders who paved way for all of us to learn, it would not have been possible for me to write this book, which primarily relied on secondary and tertiary information, analysis, and anecdotal evidence from these many sources. I express my sincere gratitude to each one of them.

Every effort has been made to give credit where it is due for the material contained herein. If inadvertently, we have missed to give credit, future publications will give due credit to those that are brought to the author's attention.

I must express heartful thank to Mr. N. K. Verma for having faith and patience in this journey. Publisher like N. K. Verma is the real force behind all those authors who attempt to think differently.

— **Amit Sharma**

The only difference between
a rich person and poor person
is
"How they use their Time."

Everyone gets the same 24 hours each day.

Be it, Albert Einstein, Mother Teresa, Isaac Newton, Narendra Modi.

They all had 24 hours a day, just like you and me.

What enabled them to lead such significant lives?

They managed their time well.

Yes. "Time Management is Life Management."
Time Management is Key to
Happiness & Success.

Until we can manage **TIME,**
We can manage **NOTHING ELSE.**

- **Peter F. Drucker**

Contents

Authors' note		13
Preface		21
1.	**Audit Your Time – Keep Time Log** Know how you spend your time - Check out where your time is going	47
2.	**Urgent are not important, and Important are never urgent** Understand what is Important and what is Urgent	53
3.	**Plan Your Work, and then Work on Your Plan**	57
4.	**SMARTER Goal** Setting Clear Goals	62
5.	**Invest TIME to Save TIME**	73
6.	**Pareto's principle – 80-20 Rule** Focus on Important tasks rather on tasks not making much difference	76
7.	**Avoid waste of time & efforts** Communicate Clearly to avoid Re-doing	80
8.	**Priority not Preference** Prioritise work, not your Preference of work	82
9.	**Preparation and Planning is Important** Plan your day in advance	85
10.	**Parkinson's Law** A bureaucratic evil that we all follow	89
11.	**Biological Prime Time** Manage your Energy to make Time productive	94

12.	**Don't let perfection be a curse**
	They did not want it Perfect, they wanted it on good enough, and on Yesterday 100
13.	**Procrast-I-nation – Nationwide problem**
	We all are natural Procrastinator. 106
14.	**Learn to Say No**
	Many a times, No is better than Yes 112
15.	**Start Your Day with MIT**
	MIT – Most Important Task 118
16.	**When being "helpful" is actually hurting**
	Say "No" and Delegate or Outsource 124
17.	**When Manage your Attention, Time will be managed**
	Say "No" and Delegate or Outsource 130
18.	**Let decisions happen automatically and smart decisions will happen by themselves** 138
19.	**Always see the Bigger Picture**
	Long-Term Planning yield huge rewards 142
20.	**Don't let Evil Side of Internet ruin you** 144
21.	**Group Similar Tasks Together for Awesome Time Management** 153
22.	**It is what you don't do, that matters** 163
23.	**Multitasking is a Myth** 166
24.	**Strike a balance between Work & Life** 174
25.	**Rejuvenate Yourself, Recharge Your Life** 180
26.	**On Things That Don't Matter, Don't spend much time in making decision – Be real Quick** 186
27.	**Commute Time is Your Think Time**
	Time is valuable only when you add value to it 188
28.	**Eliminate Distractions** 196
29.	**Use Technology for our Disposal**
	Don't become slave of Technology 204
30.	**Focus on your Physical & Mental Health** 208

Authors' note

"Time management" sounds like a simple concept, but it isn't. Almost 99% of people in this world struggle to manage their time at its best.

The Value of Time

You may have seen this popular, uncredited message that has widely circulated on the Internet or WhatsApp.

1. To realize the value of one year, ask a student who failed in his annual exam.
2. To realize the value of one month, ask a mother who gave birth to a premature baby.
3. To realize the value of one week, ask the editor of a weekly newspaper.
4. To realize the value of one hour, ask the lovers who are waiting to meet.
5. To realize the value of one second, ask the person who just avoided a traffic accident.
6. To realize the value of one millisecond, ask the person who was beaten in race by a Winner in Olympic.

How the math of betterment works out in life, how we can get better with minimal but consistent effort? In his book 'Atomic Habits' James Clear has clearly defined an interesting calculation:

- If you can get 1 percent better each day for one year, you'll end up thirty-seven times better by the time you're done.
- Conversely, if you get 1 percent worse each day for one year, you'll decline nearly down to zero.

What starts as a small win or a minor setback accumulates into something much more.

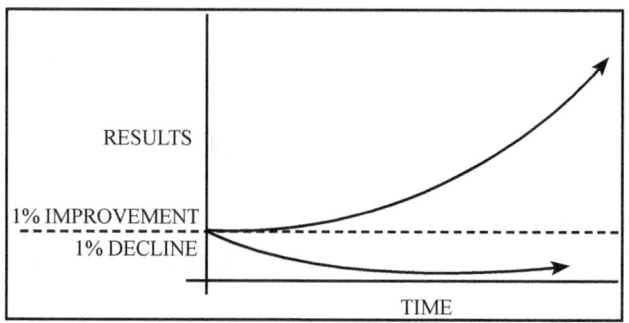

1% Better Every Day Calculation
1% worse every day for one year $(0.99)^{365}$ =   00.03
1% better every day for one year $(1.01)^{365}$ =   37.78

Numerous books and articles have been published on time management. So you might ask, 'Why another book on the subject?' At the same time, many time-management programmes have been conducted. But the return on investment (ROI) from a high percentage of these has been quite low. Two factors in particular have contributed to this:

1. They assumed that participants had control of their own roles. Yet most people's time is governed by other people's demands and superiors' priorities can change with head-spinning speed.
2. Many workshops were designed around a package rather than the specific needs of the participants. They focused on the 'how to'. But what works with one type of personality may not work with another.

Effective time management does not result from the application of an inflexible set of principles or techniques. People are different. Understanding yourself is essential for effective time management. To be able to plan your future, you have to be able to anticipate your behaviour in future situations. This requires self-knowledge.

Many of us know our particular time bandits but to change one's time-management behaviour one has to do so. Because of changes in the global economy, the need to discard old habits and adopt new and more efficient ones has never been greater.

Time has a value greater than any currency. We may leave our children the money we don't use in our own lifetimes, but we cannot leave them one millisecond of time. This makes Time Management is an important skill and habit to develop by everyone.

Time is one of the life's most valuable possessions, as it is something you can never get back. Subsequently, one of the most essential life skills to master is time management. After all, **time management is really life management.**

Mastering time management does more than just increasing productivity. It can yield important health benefits as well. When time is managed wisely, it minimizes stress and improves the overall quality of your life, which is one of the most worrisome issues in today's world.

Time Management lay the foundation for the quality of life we all dream of

Delegating the appropriate amount of time to get adequate sleep, maintain a healthy diet and exercising regularly are all essential elements to improve both focus and concentration. Making the time to create a healthy lifestyle will help improve your efficiency throughout the day, allowing for more time to complete other tasks.

There are so many distractions in this digital age we live in. As such, it's becoming harder and harder for students to master the art of time management. Of course, this doesn't mean that it's impossible to be a productive student. It just means that it'll require small effort on your part.

- Effort to get rid of old habits.
- Effort to form new habits.
- Effort to keep on trying, even when you feel like you'll never be a focused student.

By picking this book, you have already started to journey which will change your course of future, with a future full of happiness, success, stress-free life. With each page of this book, you are not only reading a book, you are just making your commitment stronger to yourself about a great future ahead. You just need to keep faith in yourself and put in the necessary efforts inline to the Time Management principles mentioned in this book.

And trust, this is very easy for you, and reward is huge.

This is not **a how-to book**. Time Management skill is a Cognitive skill, and the cognitive errors are far too ingrained within us to be able to rid ourselves of them completely. Silencing them would require superhuman willpower, but necessary for leading a good & balanced life which every human dream of and indeed deserve on this planet. Although, this book may not hold all the keys to happiness, at the very least it acts as an insurance against too much self-induced unhappiness.

This book is the result of a deep interest by both the authors in this topic. It is based on the premise that it is important to know yourself before you start to manage, how you deal with time. You cannot really manage time because it is constant, and you cannot do anything to increase or decrease the number of hours in a day. All you can do is manage yourself in relation to the amount of time you have at your disposal. Time is the great equalizer: we all have 24 hours a day, no matter how much money we have and regardless of our race, religion, creed, colour, age, and position or status in society. The skills with which the book deals are those we did not learn in school, college or university. Yet they are the skills that are essential for success in business. Today all these skills are as basic as reading, writing, and listening. In this book, you will find them all clearly and helpfully described. Read about them, study them, practise them, and soon you will be taking control of your life and your time.

Indeed, my wish is quite simple: if we could learn to recognise and learn helpful tricks of time management – in our academic lives, even in all stages of our lives whether in private lives, at work or in government – we might experience a leap in prosperity. To follow the tricks of time management in this, we need no extra cunningness, no new ideas, no unnecessary gadgets, no frantic hyperactivity – all we need is to think about the purpose of our life and see, time management is a tool to smoothly travel the beautiful journey of life.

Specially to students, apply the tricks mentioned in this book, and you'll be on your way to becoming a successful student. More than that, you would develop the skills and habits that will enable you to make a greater contribution to society over the long run.

We wish you all the best on this meaningful journey!

— **Rinkal Sharma & Amit Sharma**

Time is inelastic; it cannot be stretched.
Time is indispensable; all work and accomplishment requires it.
Time is irreplaceable; there is no substitute for it.
And time is perishable; it cannot be saved, preserved or stored.
Once it is gone, it is gone forever.

The Cycle of Improvement

1. Awareness - identify what you need to improve.
2. Deliberate practice - focus your conscious effort on the specific area you want to improve.
3. Habit - with practice, the effortful becomes automatic.
4. Repeat - begin again.

"If I wait to be Happy
I will wait Forever
If I am Happy now
I will be Happy FOREVER…"

Preface

"Sometimes questions are more important than answers."

— **Nancy Willard**

We've all heard ourselves saying it: "There's never enough time!"

Let's think about your work/life situation today, especially as it affects your time. If you're like most people, your home, car, and office are loaded with modern tools and data resources. You can stay on top of world news at every moment, reacting quickly to any problem or opportunity that may arise. With all modern technologies available for our disposal, ideally, we should be in better control of time in the current 21st Century in this digital age.

But, does the same happen with most of us? No….never. We all need to question ourselves below three questions first, to understand clearly what is real problem.

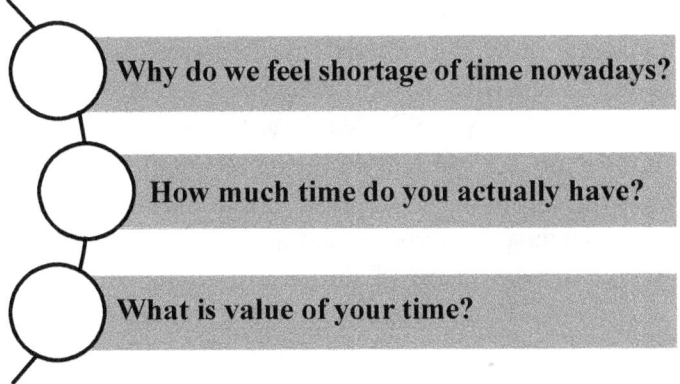

Time Management is Life Management

Q1. Shortage of time in 21st Century

Have you ever wondered, why our ancestors never needed to do time management? Why do we need it anyway? Did our ancestors get 48 hours every day and we only get 24 hours a day only? But since the beginning of the 20th century, we are facing scarcity of time and this problem keeps on increasing day by day. It has rather invented so many fast devices.

We often get irritated, provoked, tense or lose our temper when we are not able to finish our work on time. We are always in hurry because of lack of time. Due to this, our blood pressure increases, our relationships suffer, our mental balance gets disturbed and sometimes even accidents occur. The fact is that shortage of time has become an unpleasant but unavoidable part of our lives. Have you ever thought, why we feel such a shortage of time nowadays?

Before 20th century, we had no cars, bikes or scooters but our ancestors were in no hurry to reach anywhere. Earlier, there were no mixers, food processors or microwaves but housewives were not in any hurry while cooking on earthen stoves or grinding spices on stone-slab earlier. There was no electricity, **yet there was no need to work till late at night**. Actually, life was quite easy at that time because then human life was not at the mercy of a clock. After industrial age as the trend of jobs started picking up, human beings became slaves of the watch.

Earlier life was easy but now it has become quite complicated. This is, actually, the basic cause of our problems. Earlier pace of life was quite slow but now it has increased. Now Internet has entered in to our lives which connects us to the whole world in just a blink of the eye. Now we have access to TV and just by switching it on we get to know everything that happens in the whole world. Now we have 4G mobile phones which enable us to communicate with anybody and do video calling also. The modern gadgets have changed the speed of our life. Perhaps modern inventions are also responsible for lack of time in our life. They have connected us to the outside world but they have distanced us from ourselves.

If you are serious about the maximum utilisation of your time, the best solution is to get rid of all the modern inventions and adopt the old life style. It will be more convenient for you. No, I am not suggesting that you cook food on an earthen stove nor I am asking you to walk from Mumbai to Delhi on foot. Rather I would suggest that we should reduce the use of these modern technologies and make effective use only. TV, Internet, mobile phone, chatting and unnecessary surfing on Internet etc., which often is responsible for wasting our precious time.

Earlier time didn't get on our nerves and the simplest reason was that most of the people did not have a watch in those days. Earlier even the alarm clock was not needed. The crowing of the cock was enough to awake people up. At that time, there was no tension of catching metro rail or local train. At that time, it hardly matter whether people finished their work at 9 of 9.15 but today, it matters a lot.

So, before reading this book any further, please understand that lack of time is also a modern day malady like other life style related diseases namely diabetes, blood pressure (High/Low), cholesterol, and ailments of heart, etc. If you want a solution to this problem, you will have to change your life style.

Remember that the world will not change for you. It is you who has to change. If you change your life style and attitude, the equation of time will also change.

"The clock, not the steam engine, is the key machine of the modern industrial age."

— **Lewis Mumford**

Q2. How much time do you actually have?

God has bestowed some with more beauty and some with less; some with more intellect and some with less. Some people have got more wealth and some have got less. But, the wonderful thing is that everyone has got the same amount of time, i.e. 24 hours a day.

Don't say you don't have enough time. You have exactly the same number.

"A year from now you will wish you had started today."

— **Karen Lamb**

Time is the only wealth which you can not deposit in the bank. Passing time is not in your control. It keeps on slipping from your hands with each movement of the hands of a clock. What remains in your hands is only how you utilise your time. If you utilise it well, the consequences would be equally good but if you misuse it, the consequences will be bad.

Actually, we don't have much time at our disposal. The fact is that we have absolutely no control over a big chunk of our day time – 24 hours. We spend eight hours in sleeping and two hours in eating-drinking, getting ready and doing other daily routine activities. In this way, we have merely 14 hours in our hands. In other words, **only 58% of our total time is in our control while 42% of our time is beyond our control**. For the sake of convenience, we can assume that 40% of our time is beyond our control whereas, 60% of our time is under our control.

Time is valuable because it is the only thing in the world which is limited. If you lose your wealth, you can earn it again. If you lose your home, you can get it again. But if you lose your time, then you can not get it back. We have very less time and that too is limited. If we assume our life expectancy to be 80 years (in today's world and thanks to current lifestyle, life expectancy has reduced from 100 to 80 years) then we have 29,200 days in all in our life. You may count how many days are left with you to achieve your goal in life. Find out the remaining days of your life with a simple method given below.

Total Days of Life	=	29,200
The days spent (Your age X 365)	=	....
The remaining days	=	....

If we want to become something great, accomplish something big and achieve some significant goal, then it is necessary that we learn to make the best use of our time so that in this limited time that we have on earth, we may achieve everything we wish to achieve, be it wealth, fame, happiness or success.

"Time is the coin of your life. It is the only coin you have, and only you can determine how it will be spent. Be careful lest you let other people spend it for you."

— Carl Sandburg

Q3. What is value of my time?

If we start exchanging our time with money, then will we be spending our time in similar fashion like we do now? I think.... we never.

Assume that your 1 hour cost is INR 500, and you have to exchange money in proportion to time you spend.

Will you still waste your time to watch any TV serial for 1 hour, if you realize that for this 1 hour, you are actually spending INR 500, not just one hour.

None of us would do same, if we think in same way

It is often said that time is money. But this saying is not completely true. The truth is that this wealth is only prospective wealth or potential wealth. If you utilise your time well, only then you may earn wealth. On the other hand, if you misuse your time, you may lose the prospect of earning money.

Do we all accurately know how much precious or valuable our time is? If not, then use the following formula to know it.

The value of your one hour = Your income/Your working hours

By dividing your income by your working hours, you will come to know the actual worth of your one hour at present. Assume that you can earn Rs 40,000 a month and for that you the worth of your one hour will be : Rs 200.

Monthly Salary	=	INR 40,000
Working Hours per day	=	8
Working days in Month	=	25
Value of 1 Hour	=	40,000/(25*8) Coming to INR 200

According to the above mentioned example, If you are wasting 2 hours every day, it means you are losing Rs 73,000 per year. By practicing the same calculation, you will get to the revelation – your eyes must open.

> Firstly, you will come to know how much financial loss you are facing; and you will not waste time anymore.
> Secondly, you will get to realise whether value of your one hour is satisfactory or not. If it is not satisfactory, obviously you will have to find out other ways to increase its worth.

By using this formula just once, there will be a miraculous change in your life. You will become alert about the utilisation of your time. You will stop wasting it. You will start searching for ways to do more work in less time. All this will be possible only when you will realise how valuable each minute of your time is and how much financial loss is happening to you.

"The future is something which everyone reaches at the rate of 60 minutes an hour, whatever he does, whoever he is."

— **C.S. Lewis**

Why Time Management is Important

If you aren't fully clear on why time management is important, you probably won't have the motivation that is needed to change your ways. Below are the five reasons, why it's important and beneficial to learn how to manage your time well.

1. Time Management Increases Your Productivity and Efficiency

Think about everything that you somehow get accomplished when a deadline is nearing. Now think about how much higher the quality of your work could be if you weren't pushed to cut corners with a looming deadline. If you plan your time wisely, you won't be rushing through it, but with smaller deadlines, you will still feel the motivation to make progress. This pressing motivation coupled with the allowance of a reasonable pace will help you create impressive work.

2. You Gain a Sense of Fulfilment

Once your time management efforts start to pay off in the form of accomplishments, you will feel more fulfilled by your performance. Effective time management skills will also help you lead a more fulfilling life, as you will have more time to explore various opportunities that you let pass you by in the past.

If you're constantly rushing from one project to the next, you never get the chance to do the things that you may find to be truly rewarding outside of work, such as volunteering or helping someone in need. These tasks are innately fulfilling and can add enrichment to your life. Doing things that you enjoy and believe it is important in life, is actually make your time well spent.

3. You Relieve Stress

Managing your time can have a direct impact on your stress level. You will face fewer surprises, reduce your tight deadlines, and eliminate your frequent rushing from one task to the next.

If you feel like you're constantly busy but get little accomplished, or you're never able to complete your work, you're probably experiencing stress. Time management skills can help you gain a sense of control over your time, which will help reduce this pressure. As you improve your ability to meet your deadlines, you will be better equipped to stay calm while you're working. When you can manage your time well, you gain some peace of mind.

4. It Improves Self-Discipline

If you are good at managing your time, you're probably also very self-disciplined and tend to stay on track with your deadlines and goals. Having this sense of self-discipline benefits you in every area of your life, from your health, to your relationships, to your career. The more you practice time management, the better your sense of self-discipline will develop, which will increase your success at attaining goals in any area of your life.

5. Improves Your Ability to Make Quality Decisions

Planning your time wisely will help increase your productivity and efficiency.

Having good time management skills help reduce stress and allows you to set aside enough time each night to get a proper sleep. Getting ample rest has a strong impact on the quality of your decisions and can impact almost every area of your life, both personal and professional. By having effective time management skills, you can refrain from making the poor decisions that you could make during periods of stress, pressure, and fatigue.

Having sufficient time to make decisions will also allow you to be more organized and experience fewer mistakes. The more you forget details or do things incorrectly, the more work you're creating for yourself. When you're able to make good decisions in the first place, you can eliminate the need to do a task more than once.

"The first principle is that you must not fool yourself—and you are the easiest person to fool.

— Richard Feynman

Time management styles – Which Style suits to you?

Not all time management techniques are suitable for everyone.

We don't all work the same, so we don't all face the same time management issues. Everyone has a prevailing time management method of dealing with work, i.e. a time management style, one that brings its own time management issues - if you think about it, you may find that you're a:

Time Martyer	Procrastinator	Distractor
Underestimator	Firefighter	Perfectionist

1. Time Martyr

You fill your schedules with requests from others, instead of focusing on what's important to you. Your own tasks feel like too much responsibility, so you jump at the chance to take on anything else - you gain validation from others, but neglect the tasks that would bring you self-validation.

Issues: multitasking, missed deadlines, ineffective scheduling, skipping breaks

2. Procrastinator

Time Martyrs at least tackle other people's tasks - Procrastinators delay work on everything remotely important to anyone. Some claim they work better under pressure, but the results they get are often dampened by the stress and anxiety this practice brings.

Issues: missed deadlines, ineffective scheduling, multitasking

"Excuses cost a dime and that's why the poor could afford a lot of it."

— **Robert Kiyosaki**

3. Distractor

Your heart's in the right place, but you're easily distracted. A random request from a colleague is as likely to catch your fleeting attention as is a 20-minute phone call from your proprietor.

Issues: multitasking, missed deadlines, ineffective scheduling

4. Underestimator

You estimate that handling a task will take you much less than it actually does - you rarely live up to your optimistic deadlines.

Issues: missed deadlines, ineffective scheduling

5. Firefighter

You try to tackle everything on your own, right now - you're constantly putting out "fires" left and right, and don't feel fulfilled unless you're working on 10 tasks at once, and feeling "busy". Once you're done with that, you simply ask: "What's next?" - which is a practice that will lead you to burnout, sooner or later.

Issues: missed deadlines, skipping breaks, ineffective scheduling

6. Perfectionist

You're similar to the procrastinator and distractor, but your inability to finish a task at least has a noble cause - you want everything to be perfect. You'll work overtime, and invest all your efforts into delivering a high-quality project - but you often don't know how to quit while you're ahead, so you may miss your deadlines and risk burnout.

Issues: missed deadlines, skipping breaks

All the issues listed alongside your time management styles can be solved, and all the necessary time management skills can be perfected, if you only choose the right time management.

I find so many people struggling, often working harder, simply because they cling to old ideas. They want things to be the way they were; they resist change. Old ideas are their biggest liability.

It is a liability simply because they fail to realize that while that idea or way of doing something was an asset yesterday, yesterday is gone."

"The most efficient way to live reasonably is every morning to make a plan of one's day and every night to examine the results obtained."

— **Alexis Carrel**

It is about controlling the use of the most valuable - and undervalued - resource. It is managing oneself in relation to time. It is setting priorities and taking charge of the situation and time utilization. It means changing those habits or activities that cause wastage of time. It is being willing to adopt habits and methods to make maximum use of time.

With good time management skills one is in control of one's time, stress and energy levels. One can maintain balance between one's work and personal life. One finds enough flexibility to respond to surprises or new opportunities. It is not how much time one has, but rather the way one uses it. The bottom line is how well one manages time.

Internationally known author on time management Dr. Alec Mackenzie in his book "The Time Trap" argues that the very idea of time management is a misnomer because one really cannot manage time in the way other resources can be managed: financial capital, physical capital, human capital, information and time. While each of the first four can be augmented, reduced, transferred or otherwise controlled, Time cannot be manipulated. Dr. Mackenzie contends that when it comes to time, one can only manage oneself in relation to it. One cannot control time as one can control other resources – one can only control how one uses it. In the world in which we live, time cannot be replaced or re-created. It is therefore not for us to choose whether we spend or save time but to choose only how we spend it.

> ➤ People think that the faster you get something done the better. This is sometimes the case. However, you want to also make sure the job gets done with as little mistakes possible. Rushing something creates more margins for error. Spend more time on your task so that you do not have to go back and correct mistakes. Doing something on the first try and with an adequate level of quality will save your time in the long run.

- Some think that taking breaks wastes your time. While you do not want to fall prey to distractions taking a break every now and then is good for productivity. Avoid taking overly frequent breaks but make sure you divide your day up in a manner that will not put you down.
- Another misconception about time management is that you should always finish a task no matter how long it takes. While this seems like a good practice some tasks can take a large amount of time. If you have a task that will only take an hour then it is a good idea to complete it before moving to another task. However, if you have something that takes four hours you may want to split the task into smaller goals and work on them during a set period of time.
- People think that being a good multitasker is a great time saver. This may be true in some instances but it is typically better to devote all of your attention to the task at hand. That is why it is good to set aside blocks of time to complete a task so that you are only focused on the task in question. You could do a self-experiment at home and compare how much faster you get something done when you focus on it compared to when you are doing other tasks at the same time.
- I can keep all my time managed myself. While most of us would love to believe that this is true it simply is not. Relying on other things to help manage your time is a must especially in a busy work environment. Use things like appointment scheduling software to help you with planning and appointment keeping.

Time Management Facts and Figures

1. 80% of "crisis management" events are preventable.
2. One hour of planning will save 10 hours of doing.
3. Good time managers do not allocate their time to those who "demand" it, but rather to those who "deserve" it.
4. The most powerful word in our time management vocabulary is "no".

5. Delegation is an unlimited method to multiply time for achieving results.
6. The hardest part about delegation is simply letting go "If you want a job done right, you have to do it yourself."
7. Nine out of 10 people daydream in meetings.
8. 60% of meeting attendees take notes to appear as if they are listening. When someone is asking for our time for a meeting, 80% of the time there is an alternate date and time that will be acceptable.
9. The average person gets one interruption every eight minutes, or approximately seven an hour or 50-60 per day. The average interruption takes five minutes, totalling about four hours, or 50% of the average workday. 80% of those interruptions are typically rated as "little value" or "no value" creating approximately three hours of wasted time per day. 20% of the average workday is spent on "crucial" and "important" things, while 80% of the average workday is spent on things that have "little value" or "no value".
10. In the last 20 years, working time has increased by 15% and leisure time has decreased by 33%.
11. A person who works with a "messy" or cluttered desk spends, on average, 1-1/2 hours per day looking for things or being distracted by things, or approximately 7-1/2 hours per workweek. "Out of sight; out of mind." When it's in sight, it's in mind.
12. The average worker sends and receives 190 messages per day.
13. The average person today receives more information on a daily basis, than the average person received in a lifetime in 1900.
14. 70% of business and professional people use a "to-do" list on a regular basis to administer their "have to's".
15. The average reading speed is approximately 200 words per minute. The average working person reads two hours per day. A speed reading course that will improve the reading rate to 400 words per minute will save an hour per day.

16. We retain 10% of what we read. We retain 20% of what we hear. We retain 30% of what we see. We retain 50% of what we hear and see. We retain 70% of what we say.
17. We retain 90% of what we do.
18. Taking five minutes per day, five days per week to improve one's job will create 1,200 little improvements to a job over a five-year period.

Misconceptions about Time Management

There are several misconceptions which we all have about time. They affect everyone including those persons who may be considered quite successful and effective. Here are some of the misconceptions:

1. **Time management is simple.** All it requires is common sense. While it is true that the concept is simple, the self-discipline required to practice effective time management is not easy.
2. **Work is best performed under pressure.** Psychological studies show this to be no more than an excuse for procrastination. One does not work well under pressure - only does the best one can under the circumstances. Pressure and challenge must not be confused. Brian Lara's performance when the West Indies Team is in trouble has more to do with application and determination rather than pressure.
3. **I keep a diary, a to-do list and have a secretary to keep me organized.** One has to keep oneself organized - no one can do it for others. The trouble with the disorganized person is that he hardly has time to listen to his secretary or look at his diary.
4. **I do not have the time.** The effective worker or manager often gets more work done in the earlier hours of the morning than most laggards get done in the whole day. He then no longer has to work against tight deadlines and under stress which contributes to heart problems and not unusually the ultimate reduction of time on this earth.

5. **Time management might be good for some kinds of work but my job is creative.** Time management is not about routine; it is about self-discipline. Lack of discipline prevents one from being great instead of simply good.
6. **Time management takes away the fun and freedom of spontaneity.** Is working under stress, forgetting appointments, making constant excuses and apologies to be fun? Would it not be much more fun if by better organization one had one or two more hours every day to spend with the family, to play games, read a good book, plan for tomorrow and the day and week after or just relax?

> "You get to decide where your time goes. You can either spend it moving forward, or you can spend it putting out fires. You decide. And if you don't decide, others will decide for you."
>
> — Tony Morgan

7. **Let External Events Control your Day**

When you make every external event a priority, you're giving up control. If you wish to make every interruption, the center of your day, you'll get little done. So, what can you do? First realize what you can and cannot control. You can't control a car accident that's one mile ahead, and makes you late for a face-to-face with a client. But you can anticipate the future by understanding external demands and how you can react to them. In other words, build in time for the unexpected. For instance, in traffic jams, carry a cell phone and contact your client as soon as possible about the delay. Want to be even more proactive? Ask your client if the delay will inconvenience them and if they would like to reschedule. Unexpected trip to the dentist? While waiting take what you can do on the road with you. Catch up on client email or reorganize your to-do list. In other words, it may have been unexpected, but you can still utilize the time to your best ability. You can't do much to prevent traffic or a chipped crown, but you can mitigate its results.

8. **Do Not Dictate Limits**

We hear a lot about "work-life balance". In fact, numerous blogs have been written about how to say the magic word "no" when it comes to using time to its best advantage. There are a myriad of reasons why you may feel compelled to say 'yes' to every client or project, even when you know that it may not be in your best interest or your client's best interest. Understanding your motivation behind the constant need to please is half the battle. The other half is changing your behavior. It's not just what you say, but "how" you say it that results in more productivity and more time.

Bottom line: when you respect or value your time, so will your clients.

9. Everything is a Priority

As a consultant, there will be days you'll feel tempted to treat every inquiry and every set back as an immediate priority. Here is where taking a bit of time to plan and organize can go a long way. If tools work, then use them. Whether it's an online calendar or a simple to-do list use what keeps you effective. More importantly take the time to evaluate your goals and then set a realistic time to each one. The key here is the word realistic. Taking a cue from item #7, build in time for interruptions, reviews or even research for any one project.

10. Over-Scheduling Helps you Keep on Top of Things

Whether it's an evernote or outlook with calendar or an excel spreadsheet that handles the management of freelance projects, don't spend so much time planning that there is little room for the work itself. Leave a little wiggle room for flexibility in your to-do lists or your goal lists for possible revision. Prioritizing tasks or goals over and over again should be given, and is something you'll find yourself doing throughout your day.

11. Commit to Every Task Yourself

It sounds super heroic to take on every task yourself, no matter how mundane. While for others, it's simply too difficult to let go. I hate to quote from an episode of Seinfeld, but to effectively remain master of your domain; you must learn the fine art of delegation which can take you further than going it alone. Whenever necessary eliminate processes that see little to no results, or outsource tasks to others. Delegation gives you freedom. Most of all, it gives you time to grow your business and do what you've originally set out to do in the first place; be the boss.

12. Achieve Perfection Wherever and Whenever Possible

When you hang on to ideas of perfectionism, you quickly lose focus of the big picture. This may require a little rewiring in the way you think about everyday tasks. For example, consider labeling all documents or forms as a draft. Why? Because change is inevitable. By looking at documents you use every day in a slightly different way, you can reduce the pressure to produce a piece of perfection each time it comes up for revision.

13. Complete Each Task No Matter How Long it Takes

This myth also coincides with the misconception of not scheduling time to mundane tasks. But when you restrict the amount of time you give to your inbox, say one hour each day, it frees you to move on to another task or the next task on your list once the hour is over. For tasks that take longer than 4 to 5 hours, consider breaking them into smaller tasks and put these smaller tasks into the schedule accordingly. It will be much easier and less overwhelming to handle them individually, rather than tackling the entire project all at once.

14. Don't Bother Sharing Time Saving Tips, Nobody Uses Them

If people around you understand your time management style, the more likely they are to adopt some of it as their own and in the long run make tasks and strategies run more smoothly. You're also able to carry on your day with fewer distractions.

15. Routines Block Creativity

Actually it's the exact opposite. Schedule your downtime like you would schedule the rest of your day. If you haven't done it already, schedule time with your family. Yes, I mean put that family reunion, wedding, baby shower or other family event on the calendar. Downtime prevents burnout, and so does exercise. So, go ahead and schedule it. As with everything else you do as a freelancer, staying motivated and rejuvenated means more focused productivity in the long run.

16. Don't Waste Time Getting Organized

Perhaps you've heard the saying a failure to plan is a plan to fail. Set aside a few hours to determine where your time is going, what tasks or time wasters can be eliminated or processes streamlined to increase efficiency. Stopping to document exactly where your time is going, can actually save your time in the long run. A great example is spending the time to develop templates for contracts or other documents you use over and over again, so that you're not creating them from scratch each time.

17. Save Unpleasant Tasks for Last

Whenever you save the most dreaded task for last, you've creatively hit upon a recipe for disaster. No one, I know, likes or wants to tackle a presentation at 9 PM. So get the difficult or most dreaded tasks out of the way early, and finish your day with the mundane scheduling appointments, editing contracts and other tasks that take little to no time at all. Also if you break a larger task into smaller focused tasks (see #7), you could eventually view this task as something you enjoy or at the very least, see better results.

18. Multi-Task Whenever Possible

This little gem of advice goes back to the dawn of time. Some tasks, like that client presentation I mentioned earlier, should be done with complete focus and as little distraction as possible. Just give yourself a block of time. See how fast it all comes together when you're not taking phone calls, watching the news, answering questions or catching up on emails.

"Being "busy" is not a badge of honor, it's a sign that you need to get better at time management!"

— **Mike Schmitz**

 *"A wise person does at first, what a fool does at last. Both do the same thing, only at different times."*

— **Baltasar Gracian**

Develop Healthy Relationship with Time

Time. It is arguably our most valuable commodity.

Time can't be hoarded, collected, earned, or bought with hard work, money, dignity, or our soul. It slips away whether or not we choose to pack meaning into it. Use it or lose it, so goes the saying.

'Though we all know how limited our lives are in the time-space continuum, we sometimes act like we don't know the value of time. We use words like spend, kill, or waste when we speak of how we while away the finite number of hours in each day.'

Time management systems abound and still, we flounder and falter at making the most of every sunrise. We plan for the future and neglect to cherish the present. We'd rather look back wistfully even though the future is full of hope.

And yet, for many of us, it seems there are not enough hours in a day. We paddle in paradox, limbs flailing, trading in the quality of our lives while doggedly pursuing an idealized quality of life.

We need to improve our relationship with time. (Some things may appear to be contradictory. This is a testament to the complex nature of our relationship with time.)

1. Live it Up
2. Steal it
3. Be Fierce
4. Succumb to its might
5. Call up your inner sage

Live it Up	Succumb to its Might
➤ Live in the moment. ➤ Practice love-in-action. ➤ Resist the urge to rush. ➤ Single-task.	➤ Ask for help (hire a professional or an intern or enlist a volunteer). ➤ Let chores slide (relax on the definition/expectation of clean).

➢ Do things that bring joy and require little to no effort. ➢ Say yes when you mean it. ➢ Do nothing. Instead, play.	➢ Let things be (wrinkles, jiggles, warts and all). ➢ Let go of guilt and enjoy every second.
Be Fierce	**Steal it**
➢ Do only those things that matter. ➢ Limit (not cut out completely) dawdle time. ➢ End a conversation/relationship that isn't going anywhere. ➢ Stop doing things that don't bring joy or results. ➢ Cancel a commitment. ➢ Skip a task. ➢ Silence all distractions. ➢ Choose a task or a path. Don't relent. Focus. ➢ Say no.	➢ Block out a chunk of time only for yourself. ➢ Make an appearance but don't linger. ➢ Take a vacation day. ➢ Wake up earlier/go to bed later. (Habitual lack of sleep not recommended. Better sleep is.) ➢ Delegate a task to your child (i.e. put toys away, make his or her bed, etc.). ➢ Push back a deadline. ➢ Double-task (i.e. go for a hike with a friend, an activity that takes care of two—social and physical—facets of your life).
Call up your inner sage	

➢ Take a minute to list what you'd like to accomplish while being realistic about how long each item will take to complete.
➢ Arrive late/leave early (aka swoop in/swoop out—not recommended for one-on-one meetings).
➢ Show up for things that matter.
➢ Keep doing things that work.
➢ Multi-task (laundry, dishes, Crockpot and Roomba/iRobot work well simultaneously with little drama).

Time Management is Life Management

- Take advantage of in-between times (i.e. sneak an important two-minute call between appointments, take a few minutes for micro-meditation moments).
- Respond/engage only when you're ready.
- Let efficiency increase naturally (don't force it).
- Do only those things that have an urgent deadline.
- Screen calls/scan e-mails.
- Partner with another taskmaster and take turns doing each other favors.
- Make chores fun (crank up Gloria Gaynor's I Will Survive, dance around and get some exercise in).

"Your future is created by what you do today, not tomorrow"

— Robert Kiyosaki

 ### Sole Purpose of Life is to be Happy.

Happiness Mantra 1 – Detachment and Letting Go.

We must develop the ability to detach ourselves from anything or task at a moment's notice.

Some people can concentrate and absorb in a task, but, they find it difficult to forget this first activity completely while taking on to the next activity. They have some hangover period. This only shows that we get unduly attached towards various things which actually we should not.

Note that, the world is a great training school. **The only importance of various worldly things and incidents is to give us necessary training and lessons for our growth.** They themselves are not important as such. Hence, we should only use them for our learning and growth, but, not get overly attached to them and once the purpose is served by learning necessary lesson, we should forget and discard them. Concentration and detachment should be practised simultaneously. This is what Swami Vivekananda also emphasized a lot. Ability to forget and detach from past is a great quality for achieving success in life. It is well said,

"**Though it is sometimes useful to remember, but it is often wise to forget.**"

"Time management is essentially a set of competencies. The idea is that if you can develop certain competencies, you'll be able to create quality-of-life results."

— **Stephen Covey**

18 Minutes Wisdom by Peter Bregman

The 18 minutes approach by Peter Bregman, allows us to navigate through bundle of emails, phone calls, text messages, and endless meetings that prevent us from focusing our time on things that are important. Following 18 minutes wisdom in a day, will boost not only your productivity but also set your time management & life management at its best.

- Five minutes in the morning
- One minute per hour for 8 working hour
- Five minutes in the evening

1. Five minutes in the morning

Sit down and think about what you need to do today to make it successful. Then take those things off your to-do list and schedule them into your calendar.

2. One minute per hour

Refocus. Set an alarm every hour and when it beeps, "take a deep breath and ask yourself if you spent your last hour productively".

3. Five minutes in the evening

Turn off your computer and review how the day went.

All-in-all, 18 minutes approach gives an easy insight to manage your day and have a moment to reclaim your life from distractions.

"Remember that all the time management tools in the world won't get the job done if you either don't use them or don't buckle down and get to work."

"The most efficient way to live reasonably is every morning to make a plan of one's day and every night to examine the results obtained."

— **Alexis Carrel**

Add 25th Hour to your day

We all dream to have additional time to our day. Wish we have 25 hours in a day than 24 hrs in a day. Here are some tips to help you squeeze those extra minutes out of your day. Of course, you can adapt these so that they will fit in with your situation.

1. **Get up earlier** – 6-8 hours sleep is enough. You can get additional 1 hour by waking up early by 1 hour.
1. **Watch less TV** – Every Indian on average spend 3 hours infront of TV. This is sheer waste of time. You can certainly save 1 hour from your TV time.
2. Avoid allowing others to waste your time
3. **Convert your Travel time in your productive Time** - If you don't have to drive to work, use that time to study or plan. If you do drive to work listen to a motivational tape on the way to work instead of that mindless DJ talks on FM radio.
4. Organize your work; do it systematically.
5. Make creative use of lunchtime.
6. Delegate authority, if possible.
7. Spend less time on unimportant phone calls.
8. Think first, and then do the task.
9. Do what you dream about doing, instead of just dreaming about it.
10. Work hardest when you're the most mentally alert.
11. Eliminate activities that make the smallest contributions to your life.
12. Always do the toughest jobs first.
13. Before each major act ask, "Is this really necessary?"
14. Choose interesting and constructive literature for spare time reading.

15. Learn how to sleep. Sleep soundly, then work refreshed.
16. Skip desserts.
17. Stop smoking.
18. Write notes or letters while waiting for others.
19. Combine tasks that are done in the same area.
20. Be prompt for all appointments.
21. Lay out your clothes the night before.
22. Call on specialists to do work that you cannot do efficiently.
23. Learn to read more rapidly.
24. Begin the evening hours relaxed and refreshed.
25. Avoid interruptions.
26. Avoid making a big production out of tiny tasks.
27. Search out job shortcuts.
28. Know your limitations.
29. Work to your full capacity. I know it's tough to break bad habits. However, it is necessary to make sacrifices so that your business can be successful.

Don't try to implement all of these ideas at once. Implement them one at a time and repeat them until they become a part of your daily routine.

"**Even if you're on the right track, you'll get run over if you just sit there.**"

Principle of Time Management & Life Management

Audit your Time – Keep Time Log

Know how you spend your time - Check out where your time is going

Any improvement you may be able to make to your time utilization must surely presuppose that you know where time goes in the way that you work now. **Most people define this inaccurately unless they check it out.**

Time keeps on slipping, slipping, slipping……

Just as the old song goes, our days often seem to fly by out of our control. We want to get things done. But those minutes keep slipping by. Just 10% of people feel like they have control over their days. That's why the first step in time management is all about intention, control, and understanding where your time currently goes.

Do a time audit to set your intentions and see where your time currently goes.

The same way you might get audited for your taxes, a time audit is the IRS for your schedule. The foundation of all self-improvement advice is this: you have a "bank account" of 24 hours to use each day. Wanting to make a change in your life means you currently are spending your 24-hours one way and now, you want to spend your 24-hours a different way, one that is more enjoyable or productive. Spending this time differently means:

1. You want to get a current activity completed in less time.
2. You want to replace a current activity with a new one.

Step 1 : Log How You Spend Your Time

Suppose you want to take out more time to read more daily, let's say 25 pages a day/25 minutes per day, that time needs to come from somewhere. Often, information like this would stay in our mind as a vague, "I'll squeeze the time in somewhere and figure it out later."

Time Management is Life Management

That plan would be good for a few days before our schedule always seemed to "take over" and our goal was pushed to the back burner.

Step 2 : Identify Your "Non-Negotiables" LOCKED-IN Times

Before getting into the blocks of time you can adjust to fit in a new activity, let's clear out the "mostly" non-negotiable activities that are locked in, such as,

Locked In = the time to complete the activity will remain fairly constant.

1. Sleep - Vampires aside, if you don't sleep, you die. Good sleep requires 7-8 hours a night. While we could refine sleeping time a bit such as 7 hrs or 8 specifics, let's assume this is mostly locked.
2. Eating - On an average, we spend 1 hour 30 minutes dedicated to eating food each day. There is some wiggle room here for person to person as per their habit or eating style, but let's assume 1 hour 30 minutes (eating, prep, and clean up) is mostly set.
3. Hygiene / Dress - We do not want to offend our friends and neighbours and we like to look our best. Ideally 35 minutes a day total for this is adequate.

Mission 3: Identify Your Free Time

The next step is to identify the activities that you are willing to replace, that is, your free time. This is sort of "Identify Your Lock-Ins Part 2." What's left will be your free time. The difference here is that these activities are negotiable. You may not be willing to give up watching 1 hour of TV each night, but you could. Whereas, for instance, you cannot give up sleep.

Now we have a clear view of the time.

Mission 4: Your Action Plan

Now that you have a blueprint of your schedule, your next step is to write out a list of potential new activities you want to incorporate.

By auditing your time, you will get an objective look at your schedule which will provide the customizable blueprint to implement any change in your life.

The first step you need to take is finding out where your time actually goes. You may believe that you only send 30 minutes on emails, but in reality, that task is eating-up an hour of your day.

Analyze where most of your time is devoted

Keeping a time log is a helpful way to determine how you are using your time. Start by recording what you are doing for 15 or 30 minute intervals for a week or two. Evaluate the results. Ask if you did everything that was needed; determine which tasks require the most time; determine the time of day when you are most productive; and analyze where most of your time is devoted — job, family, personal, recreation, etc.

Identifying your most time-consuming tasks and determining whether you are investing your time in the most important activities can help you to determine a course of action. In addition, having a good sense of the amount of time required for routine tasks can help you be more realistic in planning and estimating how much time is available for other activities.

There are two ways to check current practice.

The first is to estimate it—guesstimate it might be a better phrase. This is most easily done in percentage terms on a simple pie chart. Decide on the main categories of work that define your job and divide the pie chart into segments.

The second way is to use a time log to obtain a much more accurate picture—recording everything you do through the day and doing so for at least a week, longer if you can (the chore of noting things down takes only a few seconds but must be done punctiliously).

Few, if any, people keep a log without surprising themselves, and the surprises can be either that much more time is spent in some areas than you think, or that certain things take up less time than you think (or they deserve)—mainly the former. Some obvious areas for review tend to come to mind as a result.

"The quality of life is more important than life itself."
— **Alexis Carrel**

In its most basic form, a time audit consists of 3 steps:
1. Write down your intentions (i.e. How do you want to spend your time?)
2. Look at personal data on how you actually spend your time
3. Adjust, set new intentions, and track progress

For example, if you want to write a novel (intention) but you're only working on it for an hour a week (allocation), something is not right.

The same goes for your work. If your main priority is to develop software (intention), but you spend the majority of your days answering emails or in meetings (allocation), you're never going to feel like you have enough time.

Start by writing down how you'd like to spend your time each day. For example, I might say:
1. Goal 1: Write blog posts (50%)
2. Goal 2: Research and education (25%)
3. Goal 3: Client and team communication (10%)

(These intentions don't have to, and shouldn't, work out to 100% of your time.)

Next, gather as much information as you can about how you actually spend your time. You can use a few different tools and resources for this.
1. Your to-do list (app/pen and paper). If you use a to-do list app like Todoist or track your daily tasks on a pad and paper, this is one way to look at how you spent your days.
2. Calendar. You might also use your calendar to track tasks. As an added bonus, your calendar contains all of the things that usually take you away from doing meaningful work, like meetings, calls, and appointments.

Understand the Planning Fallacy so you can be realistic about what can be done in a day

One of the worst time management mistakes we can make is assuming we can do more than we can. Unfortunately, this is just human nature.

While you might be at work for 8+ hours, our research shows that the average knowledge worker—writers, developers, designers, project managers, etc…—is **only productive for 12.5 hours a week. Or, roughly 2.5 hours a day.**

Psychologists call this the planning fallacy—our bias towards being overly optimistic about how long a task will take. That's why we think our calendars look like this:

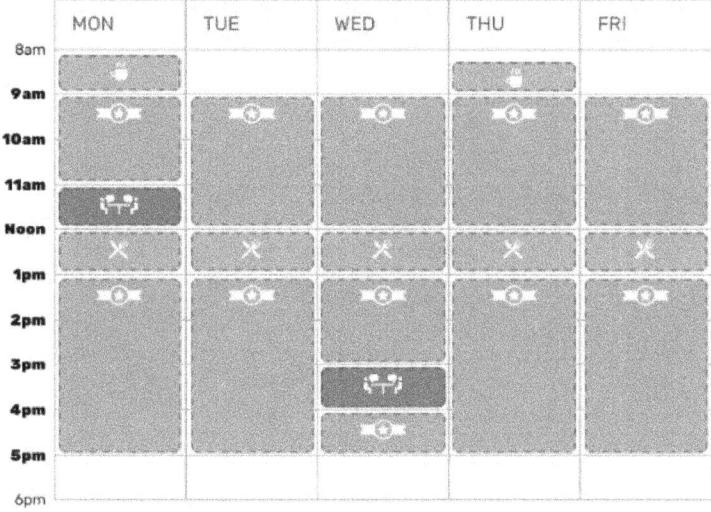

Time Management is Life Management

When a more honest one would look like this:

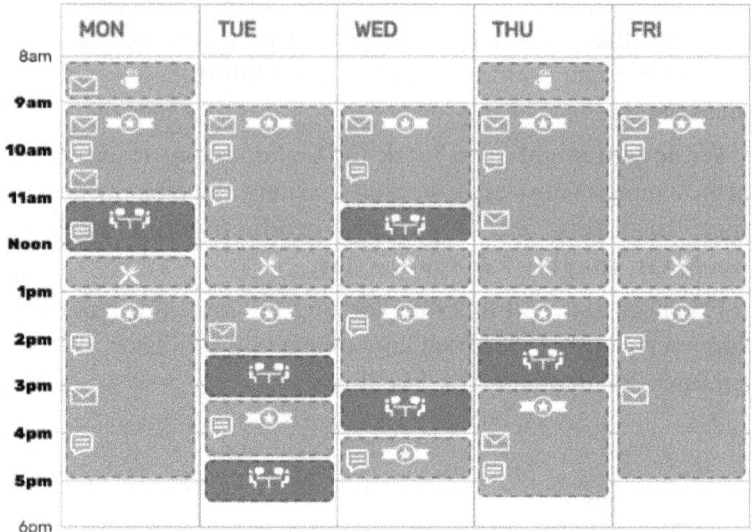

 *"Don't face complex issues head-on; first understand simple ideas deeply."*

— **Edward B. Burger and Michael Starbird**

		Principle of Time Management & Life Management
		**Urgent are not important, and Important are never urgent** Understand what is Important and what is Urgent

Activities - The urgent and the important are different in nature, yet both generate pressure to deal with them "before anything else." It can sometimes be curiously difficult to decide certain priorities. **Most people find difficult to tackle the Tyranny of THE URGENT Versus THE IMPORTANT.**

Never confuse activity with achievement.

Dwight Eisenhower, 34th US President, is identified as a man who had better control over his time and make best use of it. He once famously stated: "What is important is seldom urgent and what is urgent is seldom important." In these words, valuable secret of time management is hidden.

The question of priority is really a question of what is more important at a specific time. Priorities always involve time: what is most important to do right now. Time management is mostly a way to juggle priorities so you can meet all your goals. At the heart of time management lies prioritization of tasks, spending time on the right things and not meaninglessly meandering on things that come by.

For prioritization, we need to differentiate between tasks that are important and those that are urgent. Dwight Eisenhower came up with a matrix, now commonly referred to as the 'Eisenhower matrix' for prioritization of tasks. The matrix is divided into four quadrants, and these are explained below:

Quadrant 1 - Tasks that are urgent and important : must be taken care of immediately

For example, a house fire, emergency beeps from lab equipment, school term paper deadline, household chores, etc., be immediately attempted. But most of these tasks can be avoided with a bit of planning and organization. For example, take precautions to prevent a fire, work on term papers regularly to complete them well in advance, and follow a weekly schedule for doing household chores. **Do it now.**

	URGENT	NOT URGENT
IMPORTANT	**DO** *Do it now.* Write article for today.	**DECIDE** *Schedule a time to do it.* Exercising. Calling family and friends. Researching articles. Long-term biz strategy.
NOT IMPORTANT	**DELEGATE** *Who can do it for you?* Scheduling interviews. Booking flights. Approving comments. Answering certain emails. Sharing articles.	**DELETE** *Eliminate it.* Watching television. Checking social media. Sorting through junk mail.

Quadrant 2 – Important, but not urgent task : Need to be accomplished but have an end date or due date that isn't urgent or pressing.

These are the most important of all on which ideally the person may try to invest most of the time. For example, weekly and long-term planning, studying, developing a skill, reading books, writing a book, performing a scientific experiment, careful analysis of the experiments, writing a manuscript, etc., be attempted with a deadline. If you can do it in 2 minutes, just do it (do not schedule) – for example, writing cheque for electricity bill payment. If it takes more than 2 minutes (or if you have a more urgent thing to do), schedule it. Complete these important tasks before they become urgent as well and move to quadrant 1. Spend most of your time on this.

Quadrant 3 – Urgent, but not important task : Often feel urgent but they really aren't. Although they may feel like they need to be attended to immediately, they are not very important and can actually wait.

Some examples are help requests, text messages, phone calls, most of the emails. Consolidate such help requests (for example, colleagues requesting for a publication, etc.) so that responding to them is scheduled, rather than allowing these tasks to become frequent interruptions. Try to defer persistent interruptions as much as possible (gently apologize that you cannot help because you are doing something important). If not, try to delegate (transfer the task) to someone else. Observe brevity while responding via email or speaking on the phone. Rather than frequently checking for emails/texts (or allowing automatic notifications to interrupt you), it is suggested to schedule these tasks. For example, checking for emails and responding to them can be scheduled for twice a day, say morning and afternoon. Spend as little time as possible, and Delegate it.

Quadrant 4 – Not Important, not urgent task : Your time wasters, these things should be ignored.

For example, entertainment, playing videogames, watching TV, surfing the internet, Facebook, etc., may not be dwelled upon for a long time, just dump it.

For students who are new to time management, most of the tasks belong to Quadrants 1 and 3; for example, an assignment or term paper. As explained, most of these tasks can be completely avoided as we master managing time by scheduling the task, persistently attempting a larger project bit-by-bit every day, and by daily and weekly reviewing.

As you can see, the Urgent/Important category (#1) needs to be attended to first and should top your list of priorities, followed by the Not Urgent/Important category (#2). You can imagine that the Category #1 is a stressful place, with emergencies and crises, and one you would like to avoid. Life will bring you plenty of Category #1 items so try your best to keep things out of that category. Work productively in Category #2 so items don't unnecessarily end up being urgent. For example, a paper or a test shouldn't be urgent, as they aren't last minute crisis. The more you focus on Category #2, the more you accomplish with less stress.

Overall, the key is to think first and make considered decisions before letting particular circumstances push you into doing anything first, or just trying to do everything. Things that need action taking fast you must then either do, or delegate, at once. Things that will wait should not just be put on one side, but scheduled so that they get the time they deserve and are also completed.

In practice, the principle described above may seem difficult; indeed, it is difficult. But the difficulty is, at least in part, psychological. We usually know what is most in need of action, yet somehow the pressures of circumstances combine to give some things an "unfair"—and inappropriate—advantage and we allow that to dictate the decision and give something priority. This is a prime area where resolve is more important than technique, where there is no magic formula, and making the right judgments in a considered way must become a habit if we are to remain organized in the face of such pressures.

"Learning the art of time management helps you work smarter instead of working harder, which allows you to do more in less time."

— Ahad Gill

Principle of Time Management & Life Management

Plan Your Work, and then Work on Your Plan

The wise saying that you should "First plan your work, and then work on your plan" has formula of quality life & success. Certainly, any real progress with time management needs a plan. This must be in writing and must be reviewed and updated regularly; for most people this means a daily check.

The idea here is simply to have a written plan and regularly check and update it.

When you think for a long holiday or family vacation to a new place, what is first thing you do? – Yes, you prepare a travel plan or call it travel itinerary. So, why don't we follow same in our life journey? In today's digital world, it is important to travel through GPS navigation, likewise in life, we need plan to ensure smoother navigation.

A goal without a plan is just a wish.

Most of us have dreams of personal and professional achievements that we would love to accomplish one day, but they don't always take off because we fail to make concrete plans surrounding these visions. This is where your wishes and your goals become disconnected.

To manage our life aka time in better way, what is needed is thus sometimes called a rolling plan; not only is it updated regularly, it also provides a snapshot of your workload ahead at any particular moment. As such, it should show accurately and completely your work plan for the immediate future and give an idea of what lies beyond. As you look ahead, there will be some things that are clear a long way forward—for example, when an annual budget must be prepared and submitted; other areas are less clear and, of course, much cannot be anticipated at all in advance.

At it's simplest, such a plan is just a list of things to do. It may include:

1. A daily plan.
2. A weekly plan.
3. Commitments that occur regularly (weekly or monthly or annually).
4. A plan for the coming month (perhaps linked to a planning chart).

The exact configuration will depend on the time span across which you work. What is important is that it works for you, that it is clear, that different kinds of activity show up for what they are, and that everything links clearly to your diary and appointment system. How such a list is arranged and how you can use it to improve your work and effectiveness form part of the content of this book, but the existence of the system and the thinking that its regular review prompts is important in its own right. It is the basic factor in creating a time management discipline, and it provides much of the information from which you must make choices—what you do, delegate, delay, or ignore, in what order you tackle things, and so on. Good time management does not remove the need to make decisions of this sort, but it should make them easier and quicker to make and it should enable you to make decisions that really do help in a positive way, so that you get more done and by the best method in terms of achieving your aims.

If this is already beginning to sound like hard work, do not despair. I do not believe that the process of updating and monitoring your rolling plan will itself become an onerous task. It will vary a little day by day, and is affected by your work pattern, but on an average it is likely to take only a few minutes. I reckon I keep a good many balls in the air and am a busy person; my own paperwork on this takes perhaps five minutes a day, but—importantly—this prevents more time being taken up in less organized juggling during the day.

In practice, one point here is crucial. Some people, perhaps most, have a proportion of their day in which action is reactive. Things occur that cannot be predicted, at least individually, and a proportion of the available time is always going to go in this way.

Such activity is not automatically unimportant, and the reverse may well be true. For example, a manager on the sales or marketing side of a commercial company may have inquiries and queries coming from customers that are very important and must be dealt with promptly but will nevertheless make fitting in everything else more difficult. Sometimes the reaction to this is to believe that, because of this reactive element, it is not possible to plan, or to plan effectively. The reverse is true. If your days do consist, even in part, of this sort of random activity, it is even more important to plan, because there is inherently less time available to do the other things that the job involves and that time has to be planned even more thoroughly to maximize its effectiveness.

Also, work out what proportion of your day may be like this and then only plan other tasks to fill the time available once the reactive element is completed.

Everyone needs a plan, everyone can benefit from having a clear view of what there is to be done. If you do not have this, then the work of setting it up will take a moment, but it is worthwhile and, as has been said, it need not then take long to keep up to date. Once it is in place, you can evolve a system that suits you and that keeps up with the way in which your job and its responsibilities change over time.

1. Having a Goal is Winning Half of the Battle

Having goals in life is admirable. It shows that you want to improve your life in some way and you have hope for a better future. You're not content with the status quo. But you have to work toward your potential accomplishment for it to be anything more than an ideal.

Once you have a goal in mind, you need to break it down into clear steps you have to take in order to give yourself a sense of direction. You have to plan the what, when, where, and (most importantly) how, so you're not wandering aimlessly doing tasks that may or may not be giving you leverage to meet your goal.

When you have a goal in mind, you're in a passive "thinking" stage. But, once you have a plan, you're in an active "doing" stage. This is where you will start to make progress.

2. Your Plan is Your Key to Success

Think about what would happen if a group of builders got together to build a house, but they had no plan of action. They just started working. Without a plan, their work wouldn't be cohesive, it would be inconsistent, and it most definitely wouldn't end with a great final product.

Here are some ways a plan can benefit you:
- Help you define the extent of your project
- Determines and specifies your objectives and deadlines
- Helps you stick to a schedule (and a budget, if applicable)
- Helps you keep track of your progress
- Helps you anticipate any potential challenges, and sometimes your goals become bigger than you had originally planned once you start working, and being able to anticipate that will suppress feelings of becoming overwhelmed

Some of your goals may require more detailed and comprehensive planning than others, but having the structure of a plan will help you achieve the final product that you originally hoped for. Let's understand this with below example.

First, think about if you had a personal goal of completing a marathon.

You wouldn't just... "run more". You would develop or follow a training plan to prepare you to cross that finish line. Your training plan wouldn't have to be incredibly complex; it would just have to be a progressive strategy to get your body ready to endure that 26.2.

Aforementioned goals have necessary plans, but it's not a requirement for every goal to have an extremely extensive plan of action. Don't let the planning stage scare you off from creating your goals.

3. Where Should You Start?

Creating a sturdy action plan starts with having a clear goal in mind. Your plan will ultimately take you from your current starting point to the attainment of your goal. With a well-crafted plan, you can achieve pretty much any goal you set out to complete. But, where do you start in terms of planning?

Creating a well-crafted plan will help you achieve pretty much any goal you set out to complete.

Writing

A 2015 study found that people who commit their plans in writing are 33% more likely to achieve their goals. And, in recent years, writing plans for achieving goals in reverse has gained popularity. But why does reverse planning lead to increased motivation, higher expectancy of achieving one's goal, and a reduced feeling of time pressure?

There are three possible reasons for this:

- ➢ Focusing on the end goal helps you imagine future events as if they've already occurred. This makes it easier to visualize exactly what you need to do to get there. "Future retrospection" amps up your anticipation of success, which evokes goal-oriented behaviors.
- ➢ Backward planning helps you focus on a positive outcome. The entire time you're planning, you have in mind that you have already achieved your goal, which makes the steps leading up to that moment a no-brainer. Alternatively, when you plan a goal from the beginning to end, you have a higher chance of feeling intimidated as you start to think about the obstacles you may face in the process.
- ➢ Planning backward helps keep your motivation high. Everyone's motivation is usually at its peak at the beginning and closes to the end of a project. Reverse planning gives you a map to the completion of your goal by outlining every step you have to take along the way. This can help you maintain your focus for the duration of the project, even when your enthusiasm may otherwise start to diminish.

"Time today seems to be a bit more difficult to manage. This is because of the development of new devices that can keep anyone connected with friends, work, and other important or non-important things."

— **Richard Carroll**

Principle of Time Management & Life Management

SMARTER Goal
Setting Clear Goals

Any plan is, in turn, as good as the objectives that lie behind it.

So it is to objectives, certainly a fundamental factor affecting the management of time.

Always set Clear Goals

Goal setting is a key component of time management. Setting goals allows you to align your activities with the big picture results you're working toward. Goals provide clarity, purpose, and meaning at work. If you want to take control of your life, it's essential to learn how to set goals and how to achieve them.

Prioritize your goals

Now prioritize for effectiveness. Remember, there's no point in doing a job efficiently if you shouldn't be doing that job at all. Think about what's really important and how much time you'll need to accomplish each goal. Then schedule an uninterrupted block of your time to do it.

Maxims advocating setting clear objectives are everywhere—for example, the idea that if you don't know where you are going any road will do.

You do need clear objectives, and they must not be vague or general hopes. Without having clearly defined goals it's easy to lose focus and direction.

Why goal setting is important

Goal setting is important as you create a clear, specific benchmark to work towards in business and life, which will help you determine whether you are being successful or not. Achievable goals that are specific and measurable can harness your emotional energy and ensure you feel confident and are motivated every day.

You can use the SMART goals system to ensure your goals are specific, measurable and achievable.

When you commit to goal setting and learn how to achieve goals, it creates powerful actions that will act as a guide to help you develop personal goals and business goals.

But, many people fall at the first hurdle when it comes to learning how to goal set.

Goal Setting – A powerful Process for thinking about and creating your ideal future

Goal setting is the act of setting clearly defined goals and then working towards goal achievement every day. These clearly defined goals should be something you want to achieve in the future with a clear date to achieve the goals by.

1. To set a goal think about something specific you want to achieve in the future – this must be a number or an event.
2. Then set a deadline for achieving the goals in.

Goal setting process – how to set defined goals

Many people, be they entrepreneurs, small business owners, leaders or managers are focused on goal setting. They talk about setting goals. But many fail to follow through and take the action needed to achieve those goals.

The reason?

They're not emotionally invested or intellectually engaged in the achievable goals. Their goals are too broad, they are not clearly defined goals, so they become less motivated to achieve the goals.

When you think about the steps to goal setting, remember the goals must be specific, a number or an event, and have a deadline attached to the goal.

How to set goals and achieve them

When setting goals, your goals should be numbers or events. They should be defined goals with a specific, measurable deadline.

When goal setting, the goals you choose must be emotionally compelling enough that you want to take action on achieving them. Otherwise, they will fall by the wayside.

Some people have goals in their mind but they're not written down or committed to.

Goal setting theory

The emotional and intellectual power you attach to each goal you set becomes the key driver of internal motivation and commitment to achieve your goals.

Imagine you want to lose some weight.

Having a goal of losing weight is too general, the goal is not clearly defined or measurable. There is not enough emotional power to push you to achieve a generic goal. To be more committed to goal achievement, ensure the goal is specific, measurable with a deadline.

The importance of setting defined goals

If you want to learn how to set and achieve goals, use this 8-step goal setting process to help you achieve your biggest goals in the next 90 days. These tips for goal setting will help you set goals that are important to you and achieve the goals much quicker.

1. Set goals by visualising your ideal future

Goal setting starts with seeing something in the future that doesn't currently exist. It is a future you that is your ideal, across your business and life. To get a true perspective of what this future looks like, visualise it in as much detail as possible. Get a sense of what it looks like, what it feels like. Then be clear with yourself on what needs to happen to make that vision a reality.

Once you create a picture of this ideal future, this is where your mindset kicks in.

The more clarity you have around the details of what goals you want to achieve, the more your mind will take ownership of the result. A goal helps you gain clarity on your direction of travel. They help you build a picture and articulate your biggest desires.

They are an anchor and guide that you can continually refer back to, ensuring you are heading in the right direction.

When setting goals be clear on exactly what you want. Be clear on when you want to achieve them by. Ensure you have clear measurements in place. I also work with clients on setting specific, measurable 90 day goals that can be continually reviewed.

Your goal setting process becomes the framework for creating the kind of bigger future you are looking to achieve.

Ensure they are your goals. They are not created or defined by anyone else. When followed day after day, they can become the foundation of your personal growth and freedom.

2. Know what goals you want to achieve

If you don't know where you're going, how will you know when you get there?

Some of the most successful entrepreneurs will build a business and personal vision 3 years into the future, 5 years into the future. Some will look 25 years into the future.

Through goal setting, they lay out exactly what goals they want to achieve and then work backwards setting defined goals that are timely and measurable.

The importance of short-term goals

In my experience setting quarterly or 90 Day goals is the key to achieving your goals, and constantly reviewing is a cornerstone of success. They are a clear 'stepping stone' towards the bigger vision but feel very achievable.

3. Write down your goals

Do you still use a pen and paper to make notes or write down your latest idea? People who actually write down their goals are more likely to have success getting to where they want to go.

There is a personal commitment at play when we physically write down our goals. A goal is embedded in your mind and subconsciously your brain is looking for every opportunity to work on achieving the goal. The written goal also gives you a place to refer back to if you are having a challenging time.

This can help you reset, get more focused and motivate you to push on towards achieving the goal.

4. Set clearly defined goals

With goal setting, it's essential that you set realistic deadlines and metrics to measure success. Your mind needs a realistic deadline to take the goal seriously. It also makes you more accountable to actually achieving the goal you've set. Otherwise, you may feel *"you'll get to it when you can"* and you won't be properly emotionally invested in the outcome or result.

> *The deadline you set for each goal should be challenging, exciting but also feel achievable.*

5. Hold yourself accountable when setting your goals

This is a big one.

If you are an individual entrepreneur you feel the weight of total responsibility on your shoulders, then holding just yourself accountable can be difficult. From my experience as a Business Coach working with successful individual business owners, I understand that accountability really is the key to success.

Working on achieving goals with a business coach or sharing your goals with peers, your family or team members provides real incentive and motivation to push forward, do what you say you'll do and really take action.

You really feel accountable and committed. It also motivates you to up your game still further and reach for things you didn't think were possible. Being held accountable pushes you further and gives you the added incentive of making things happen. It also pushes your creativity.

You will come up with new ideas, new thinking because you're surrounding yourself with someone or people you trust and respect.

6. Achieve your goals by breaking them down

We all know that learning how to goal set is just the start. It is not the end result. **The process of setting goals and achieving your**

goals should be enjoyable, stimulating and drive you forward every day. On the journey to goal achievement you should learn something new about yourself, should push yourself further.

Emotionally invest in working on goals

The more powerful your goal setting and the more emotionally invested you are in achieving them, the greater the end result.

Your progress gives you the ability to transform every aspect of your business and life based around your desired outcome. If one of your goals is to leverage your time to focus on bigger activities, then you can tangibly measure progress towards the goal every day.

Through goal setting and goal achievement, you will see the transformation in every area of your life.

7. Own your future through goal achievement

We are personally responsible for our future and must take ownership of what we can become and have belief in creating the ideal future. If you are not in control of where you spend your time and what you want to focus on, others will happily distract you.

By setting goals you are clear on what has led you to this moment.

You understand your past and have learnt lessons, both positive and negative. This helps with goal setting. There is a vision of your future with desired results so you become more in control of where you are right now in this present moment.

By sitting in the present with a clear view of your desired future you can take complete control of every aspect of your life. By achieving goals, you'll have more freedom in every area of your business and life.

8. Use goal setting in all areas of your life

Goal setting and learning how to achieve goals is not just about your study or work only. It can be the fuel for achievement in every aspect of your life, be that health, finances, relationships, fitness or personal growth.

As we have discussed the key to goal setting and achieving goals is to understand your motivation and desire for achieving them.

- Why are they important?
- What will it feel like when I achieve them?
- How will it really make a difference?

When you understand this it will play a significant role in aligning you with your goal and getting you to change some habits that are required to fully realise the goals.

Having clearly defined goals is the cornerstone to effective goal setting. Developing goals that are specific, measurable and with a deadline will ensure you are emotionally invested in achieving the goals.

Steps to Setting S.M.A.R.T.E.R. Goals

1. Step #1: "S" – Specific

The first step in setting S.M.A.R.T.E.R. goals is to be specific – very specific. The more specific you are about your goals, the better and more able you'll be to accomplish them no matter what method you use. This means that you don't just say you want to make more money or lose more weight, you have to say exactly how much money you want to make or how much weight you want to lose. You have to put a real and exact figure on it. Make it measurable.

Why is this so important? Well, in goal setting, in order to make it visceral to the mind and more clear, you have to be able to quantify that goal. Without specifics, there's no real target, just some obscure direction. When the goal is obscure, it allows the psychology of your mind to override your goals. You succumb to things like emotion-numbing activities, to easily avoid doing something that wasn't that concrete in the first place.

Specifics are the fuel in the engine of your goals. You have to provide specifics if you're going to achieve anything at all. When you write out your goals, be absolutely as specific as possible. And never be afraid to be too specific.

2. Step #2: "M" – Meaningful

The second step in setting S.M.A.R.T.E.R. goals is to set goals that are meaningful enough to you that you'll get out there and do whatever it takes to achieve them. This is the "why" in goal setting that I discussed in a prior post. When your goals have a deep enough meaning to you, you'll do whatever it takes to achieve them. This doesn't have to do with vanity or superficial reasons, but more profound and life-altering reasons why you want to achieve something.

People don't want more money because they want more paper with deceased notables on them. No, they want more money because of what that money will bring them: time, freedom, family, security, contribution, and so on. You have to attribute a strong enough meaning to your goals, beyond being just specific about them. So, next to your specific goal, write out what that goal means to you and make sure that it's something important.

3. Step #3: "A" – Achievable

The third step in setting S.M.A.R.T.E.R. goals is to set goals that are achievable. Now, there's certainly a school of thought out there that says that you can accomplish whatever you want, whenever you want it. But, when you're setting goals, especially when they're short-term goals (i.e. within 1 year), make sure that they're achievable. This doesn't mean that you can't shoot for the stars in your long-term plans, such as 5 years down the road or even 10 years down the road. It just means that you have to pick goals that you can achieve in the short term.

For example, if you've never made more than INR 10,00,000 in a year, don't say that you're going to be a billionaire in the span of one year. Set goals that you can actually achieve so that you build on your momentum. Your short-term goals should be something within your reach, but not so easily attainable that they won't take much work or effort on your part. This will also help you to build that all-important momentum. Once you achieve your year-long goals, you can broaden those into much greater hopes and dreams down the road.

4. Step #4: "R" – Relevant

The fourth step in setting S.M.A.R.T.E.R. goals is to set goals that are relevant to your life. This means that the goals should be inline with and in harmony with what you actually want out of life; they should match up with your core values. If your core values are contradicting your goals, then you'll find yourself merely getting frustrated and giving up.

When you set goals that are relevant, you have to dig deep down inside and truly understand what you want out of life. If one of your core values is freedom, then setting goals that have you bound to a desk most of the year won't help you to live a fulfilled life. Remember, your goals shouldn't be designed with the notion of succeeding to be happy, but rather, with happily succeeding. Set goals that are relevant and inline with what you truly want out of life.

5. Step #5: "T" – Time-Bound

The fifth step in setting S.M.A.R.T.E.R. goals is to ensure that they're time-bound goals. You have to set an exact date on when you plan to achieve these goals. Focus on goals that are in 3-month intervals. If you plan to achieve a 10 kg weight loss in one year, then break that down into 3-month intervals. That's 2.5 Kilogram every three months.

When your goals are time-bound, they're measurable, and you should hold yourself accountable by measuring those goals on a daily, weekly, and monthly basis. How close are you to achieving your goals? How much further did you get from achieving your goals? Without making your goals time-bound and measurable, you won't be able to see your progress.

6. Step #6: "E" – Evaluate

The sixth step in setting goals using the S.M.A.R.T.E.R. method is to ensure that your goals are evaluated. By evaluating your goals every single day, you'll be much more likely to achieve them. Why is that? Well, long-term goals (and also goals that are 3 months or 6 months out), can easily be ignored if they aren't evaluated every single day.

Make sure that you setup a system for evaluating your goals and you make the evaluation of your goals habitual. Don't ignore this all-important step. Your mind has a very clever way of allowing you to ignore your goals by pushing you into emotion-numbing behaviors when those goals aren't closely evaluated.

7. Step #7: "R" – Readjust

The final step in setting goals with the S.M.A.R.T.E.R. method is to re-adjust your approach. If, for example, you find yourself pursuing a goal but continuously hitting a brick wall, readjust your method and techniques. For example, when a plane has a goal of flying from Delhi to Mumbai, it has to constantly evaluate its progress and readjust its approach to ensure that it reaches its target. The plane constantly evaluates and readjusts until it arrives in Mumbai. You should be doing the same for your goals.

Readjust doesn't mean that you have to throw your goals out and start all over. What it means is that you have to try different approaches until you find yourself getting closer and closer to your goals. That's why constant evaluation on a daily basis is so important. If you don't evaluate you can't measure your progress.

"Time management can be learned like any other skills and don't forget that time well managed is a life well spent."

— T.P. Stone

Sole Purpose of Life is to be Happy.

Happiness Mantra 2 – Reduce emotional involvement, take things easy.

The root cause of our suffering is our emotional involvement while dealing with various incidents, situations and circumstances of life.

We should watch and tackle all worldly objects and situations objectively like a spectator as if they are different and we are different and we only have a temporary association with them.

The cause of our emotional involvement with worldly things is that we are taking them too seriously which actually we should not.

We should realise that no difficulties or problems are permanent. They all will pass. Such is the law. Everything is in a state of constant motion and change. **Nothing is permanent and static here.**

Taking things seriously also results in formation of deep impressions in your subconscious mind which result in the development of various biases and prejudices in our mind in favour of and against various things and reduces its ability to see things objectively (i.e. as they really are). In other words, emotions of like, dislike, love, hatred, jealousy, revenge etc. should be gradually rooted out, resulting in a truly unbiased and detached mind which can remain calm, serene and balanced in all the trials and odds of life.

Principle of Time Management & Life Management

Invest TIME to Save TIME

You will find that some ways of saving time, or better utilizing it, do need an investment—but it is an investment of time. **It seems like a contradiction in terms, having to spend time to save time.**

Invest time to save time.

There is a time equation that can and must be put to work if time is to be brought under control. There are many ways of ensuring that time is utilized to best effect, and, while some take only a moment, others take time either to set up or for you to adopt the habit of working in a particular way.

If we consider an example, then the point becomes clear. This is linked to delegation, a subject we return to later, and to the phrase you have perhaps said to yourself, or that at any rate is often repeated:

"It is quicker to do it myself."

When this thought comes to mind, sometimes, and certainly in the short term, the sentiment may well be correct. It is quicker to do it yourself. But beware, because this may only be true at the moment something occurs.

Say someone telephones you requesting certain information, it doesn't matter what, but imagine that you must locate and look something up, compose a brief comment to explain it, and send the information off to the other person with a note of the comment. It is a minor matter and will take you only four or five minutes.

Imagine further that, to avoid the task, you consider letting someone else do it. They are well able to, but explaining and showing them what needs to be done will certainly take 10–15 minutes of both your time and theirs. Please figure out time saving.

Time Management is Life Management

Time Taken to respond routine telephone call and action to update post telephone call	10 mins
Number of such routine calls come daily	2 calls per day
Total Time spend in a week (5-days week) for such routine task	10*2*5 = 100 min
Total Time spend in a month (24 working days in month) for such routine task	10*2*24 = 480 Mins = 8 hrs
Total Time Spend in an year (288 working days in an year) for such routine task	10*2*288 = 5760 Mins = 96 hrs = 4 days = 12 working days

Now compare above table with below calculation to see the difference. Investment of little time once is quite worth to save huge time for future. If you take the time to brief someone, then they will only have to take the action for less than a week and the time spent briefing will have paid off; thereafter you save a significant amount of time every week, indeed you save time on every occasion that similar requests are made on into the future.

Time Taken to respond routine telephone call and action to update post telephone call	10 mins
Number of such routine calls come daily	2 calls per day
Time invested to brief someone to do this routine task	30 mins
Monitor it for 5 days	30 + (10*2*5) = 130 mins

It really is quicker to do it yourself. Not so; or rather certainly not so if it is a regularly occurring task. Say it is something that happens half a dozen times a week. This is surely worthwhile.

> *The time equation here of time spent as a ratio of time saved works positively.*

In his book "Procrastinate on Purpose", author Rory Vaden proposes we allocate 30x the time it takes us to complete a task to train someone else to do it. Here's how he came to that number:

If you have a task that takes 5 minutes a day to do, budget 30x that time (so, 150 minutes) to train someone else to do it. That might seem like a huge waste of time right away, but multiply that 5 minutes a day across the 250 annual working days and you would personally be spending a staggering 1250 minutes on that task.

Taking the time to delegate and train someone else gives you a net gain of 1100 minutes a year. Or, as Vaden puts it in his book, a 733% increase in ROTI (return on time invested).

Managing your time isn't just about today, it's about setting up systems and processes that will bring you more time in the future.

This is often the case and worthwhile savings can be made by applying this principle, both to simple examples such as that just stated and to more complex matters where hours or days spent on, say, reorganizing a system or process may still pay dividends. In Practice, beware, it is so easy to fall into this trap. For whatever reason, we judge it to be possible (better?) to pause from what we are presently doing for the few moments necessary to get another task out of the way, but not for longer in order to carry out a briefing or whatever other action would rid us of the task altogether, and ultimately make a real time saving. It is worth a thought. Become determined not to be caught in this time trap and you are en route to saving a great deal of time.

"Every single one of us has a reason to manage our daily time. Managing what we do and when we do them is important in making our lives less chaotic."

— **Stephen Hall**

Time Management is Life Management

Principle of Time Management & Life Management

Pareto's principle : 80-20 Rule

Focus on important tasks rather on tasks not making much difference

You may be a massive introvert. Maybe you don't actually socialize too much, but when you do, 80 percent of your time is spent with the same 20 percent of your friends and family members.

80 percent of results will come from just 20 percent of the action.

When you draw up to-do lists, set schedules, make appointments, and so forth, chances are you're wasting most of your time.

For example, it's better to go through 10 articles in an hour (glancing over for a little more than 5 minutes) and choosing two best ones in the next hour than spending two hours reading three articles in detail. It may be a little difficult at the beginning but you're used to it, you'll see

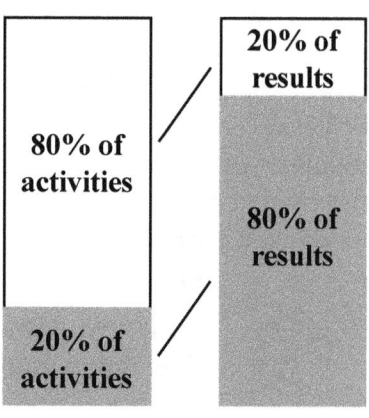

a rise in your productivity and will be able to better manage time and effort.

As per mathematical law called the Pareto Principle, which says that, in most situations, 80 percent of the effects come from 20 percent of the causes. The Pareto Principle holds sway for most work efforts that aren't purely rote. Most people obtain 80 percent of their actual results from 20 percent of their actual effort. There are many examples which validate it, ranging from wealth distribution to damage from natural disasters.

Vilfredo Federico Damaso Pareto was born in Italy in 1848. He would go on to become an important philosopher and economist. Legend has it that one day he noticed that 20 percent of the pea plants in his garden generated 80 percent of the healthy peapods. This observation caused him to think about uneven distribution. He thought about wealth, and discovered that 80 percent of the land in Italy was owned by just 20 percent of the population. He investigated different industries and found that 80 percent of production typically came from just 20 percent of the companies. The generalization became Pareto's 80/20 Rule.

This "universal truth" about the imbalance of inputs and outputs is what became known as the Pareto principle, or the 80/20 rule. While it doesn't always come to be an exact 80/20 ratio, this imbalance is often seen in various business cases.

On a more personal note, you may also be able to relate to your unintentional 80/20 habits.

1. Many of us own number of amazing suits, but 80 percent of the time or more, we grab only 2-3 suits and wear them more often.
2. I have 10 rooms in my house, but I spend about 80 percent of my time in just my bedroom, family room, and office.
3. On my smartphone, I have 48 different mobile apps pinned to the tiles, but 80 percent of the time I'm only using the eight on my home screen.

While talking and discussing many successful people, self-made millionaires, straight-A students and successful sportsperson, the productivity habits of high achievers also proves same. For them, handling every task that gets thrown their way—or even every task that they would like to handle—is impossible. They use Pareto to help them determine what is of vital importance. Then, they delegate the rest, or simply let it go.

Instead of trying to do the impossible, a Pareto approach is to truly understand which projects are most important. What are the most important goals of your or your organization, and which specific tasks do you need to focus on to align with those goals. No matter what your situation, it's important to remember that there are only so many minutes in an hour, hours in a day, and days in a week. Pareto can help you to see this is a good thing; otherwise, you'd be a slave to a never-ending list of things to do.

The idea is that most things are not distributed evenly. Does this mean that you should work any less? Not necessarily. Instead, this concept is encouraging you to focus more on the things that matter most, primarily the tasks that help us reach our goals.

Use of Pareto Principle to enhance time management

1. Rethink your to-do-lists.

With this principle in mind, this might be the time to change how you make your to-do lists. Typically, these lists consist of simple items that may not be the most important things you should be doing. Instead, your to-do lists should reflect your priorities but also take into account whether the effort necessary is worth doing.

In order to get the most out the Pareto Principle, which will help you better manage time, start by prioritizing what you need to do based on the amount of effort involved. Number these items from 1 to 10, with one requiring the least amount of effort. Then, consider the potential positive results from doing those things. Label those from 1 to 10, with 10 having the highest impact.

2. With these findings, the next step is to create a new ranking of the items on your to-do list. Divide the amount of effort by the potential results. This gives you the priority ranking you need to more effectively manage time and increase results. Those that deliver the greatest results with the least effort are complete first. Others that require more effort with little results can be postponed or removed from your to-do list.

Evaluate all of your tasks and assess your goals.

Another approach is to identify the 20 percent of your tasks that will produce 80 percent of your results. You can accomplish this by asking questions like:

1. Do I consider all of my tasks and functions urgent?
2. Am I wasting too much time on specific tasks?
3. Does this task help me reach my goals?

4. Am I the most qualified person for the job? Or, should it be completed by someone else?

After evaluating your tasks, you'll also want to assess your goals. You'll want to pay attention to the 20 percent of your activities that will help you achieve your objective. For example, you're in the 20 percent if you're working on activities that improve your life or are related to the big picture. Additionally, you're in the 20 percent if you're spending time doing the things that you enjoy and are delegating items that you're not skilled at.

Working effectively means deciding the relative priorities of different tasks. Obvious perhaps, and of course you may say some things are clearly more important than others. But, it is very easy to underestimate just how much this concept influences what you need to do, indeed just how much it influences your inherent effectiveness.

> *"Why get up early? I'd say the main reason is that you'll have a lot more time to do things that are more interesting than sleeping."*
>
> — **Steve Pavlina**

|  |  | Principle of Time Management & Life Management
Avoid waste of time & efforts
Communicate Clearly to avoid Re-doing |

Referencing an adage, there is never much time to do anything properly, but there must always be time to do it again. Nothing is more likely to end up with something having to be redone than a manager not making it clear to people what they had to do in the first place.

Communication clearly if you don't want devil of re-doing.

Always ensure that instructions are clear.

People should be clearly told -

1. **What** needs to be done (and give them sufficient details).
2. **Why** it needs to be done (knowing the objectives may make the task clearer and will improve motivation).
3. **How** it should be done (methodology etc.).
4. **When** it should be completed (and anything else about the timing).

Instructions should always include asking if everything is clear—get some feedback. Any short cut of this sequence must be on the basis of genuine knowledge or familiarity, not simply assumption that all will be well.

If the dialogue is disrupted, the consequences are usually painful. When we don't communicate properly, we simply waste time. For example, our colleague may misread our intentions and, in the worst case, do the opposite of what we expect of him/her.

Always dedicate a little while (or maybe, a bigger while) to make sure that everyone understood your instructions. This way, you will avoid unnecessary misunderstandings and minimalize the chances of the workflow being disrupted. Keep in mind a few simple things:

1. First of all, make sure that you understand what others expect from you. If the instructions are even slightly unclear, do not be afraid to ask again. Better safe than sorry!
2. When the case has the highest priority you have to obtain a written confirmation. For example, if you are planning an important meeting, send an email to those that you are planning to meet with in order to receive a confirmation of their presence.
3. The other way around – if you are the one who got invited to the meeting, at least a day before it send an email confirming your arrival.
4. **You are responsible for your way of communication!** If the task you commissioned has been done wrong, you are probably the one to be blamed. Give clear instructions!

Good, clear instructions save time, written guidelines do the same, and for some tasks they are useful; this is especially true of awkward or difficult jobs that are performed regularly but infrequently.

All instructions, in whatever form, must be clear. If you issue instructions, remember this; if you receive them—ask if necessary.

"Train your thoughts like you train your body for a marathon. Actively practice for a certain amount of time every day."

— **Louise R Allen**

		Principle of Time Management & Life Management
		**Priority not Preference** Prioritise work, not your Preference of work

Everyone likes to do what he likes

And not

What should be done

Always ensure that instructions are clear.

You ask your colleague to do something and just when you are expecting the results, you discover that he has been at something else just because he liked doing that and did not do what should have been done.

This may seem an odd one, but it is potentially even more time-wasting than putting off things that you do not like or that you find difficult. Many people spend a disproportionate amount of time on the things they like doing best and, perhaps, also do best. It is a common phenomenon in offices, and this is perfectly natural and there are various reasons for it.

Why do many individuals behave so? Simple, it is part of human nature. I believe so. But, how can we motivate? Money is not the best answer in situations. Don't just tell the individual about the activity. Show him the goal that it will help in achieving so that he not only knows the force that he has to apply but also the direction in which he has to apply it.

An important reason is that any concentration on what you like is what seems to produce the most job satisfaction. This is fine if that satisfaction comes simply from doing whatever it is and the thing itself is necessary, though the danger is that you may be prone to some over-engineering, doing more than is necessary, putting in more time and sometimes producing a standard of quality or excellence that is just not necessary.

But there can be more sinister reasons for this practice. For example, it may be because:

1. You are using one task to provide an excuse to delay or avoid others (difficult or unfamiliar things, perhaps), telling yourself, with seeming reason, that you are too busy to get to them.
2. You are concerned about delegating (a subject covered separately) and worry that a task is not a candidate for this, so you go on doing it yourself and go on over-engineering.
3. You find the work conditions of one task too tempting, such as a low-priority job that involves visiting an attractive location new to you, for instance; this is something that is compounded by the opposite being true of the priority task.
4. You find some aspect of the task fun; as an example, this happens to some people who have a fascination with computers, and they spend hours devising, say, a graphic representation of some figures when something simpler would meet the case just as well.

All these and other reasons can cause problems. The practice is frankly all too easy to engage in, we are all prone to it, probably all do it to some extent, and thus we all have to be constantly on our guard against it. Usually it continues because it is easy not to be consciously aware that it is happening.

Avoid what is sometimes called "cherry picking." The answer here is to really look, and look honestly, as you review your tasks and your regular work plan, for examples, of this happening. Better still, look for examples of where it might happen and make sure that it does not. Of all the points in this book, I would rate this as in the top few best potential time savers for most people. Do not be blind to it—it is so easy to deny it happens. Check it out and see how much time you save. And, who knows, maybe some of the extra things you can then fit in will become tomorrow's favourite tasks.

 *"Time today seems to be a bit more difficult to manage. This is because of the development of new devices that can keep anyone connected with friends, work, and other important or non-important things."*

— **Richard Carroll**

		Principle of Time Management & Life Management
		# Preparation and Planning is Important Plan your day in advance

Planning is the best, and most proven of all-time management techniques.

Firstly, because it helps to properly organize your work.

Secondly, because it gives you a detailed insight into all the things you need to do.

If you can plan your daily, weekly or monthly tasks, the rest comes easily.

Each night before you go to bed, you should create a to-do list for the following day, to keep your work in perspective. Lists are an important part of a well-structured day and making one in the morning would take away from the time you could spend on more important activities.

You can make this planning into a habit.

Every night, 10-15 minutes before going to bed, write everything you have to do on a piece of paper. While writing, think about the tasks, how long they may take, and how important they are. Determine the most important task, the one you'll tackle first thing in the morning.

By this way, you are awaking the giant within you – that is your 24X7 powerhouse, your sub-conscious mind whose power is unimaginable.

Create to-do lists

A recent study has shown that listing all the work you plan to do for the day, frees you from the anxiety over unfinished work, and makes you more effective.

First, brainstorm and create an ultimate list of everything you wish to accomplish within a time period. Once you have

Time Management is Life Management

all your activities and ideas listed in random order, streamline your schedule.
1. Organize your notes and make them into list items.
2. Group similar tasks together.
3. Single out your most important tasks.
4. Parse projects and tasks into more manageable chunks.
5. Set deadlines or time estimates on how long it should take you to finish each item on your list.
6. Check each item as you finish it, to maintain a sense of progress.

Important is to categorize your work correctly

A beautiful story provides best explanation on categorization of anything based on important. This applies to many other aspects of life as well.

> *A philosophy professor once stood before his class with a large empty jar. He filled the jar with large rocks and asked his students if the jar was full.*
>
> *The students said that yes, the jar was full.*
>
> *He then added small pebbles to the jar and asked again, "Is the jar full now?"*
>
> *The students agreed that the jar was indeed full.*
>
> *The professor then poured sand into the jar and asked again.*
>
> *The students then agreed that the jar was finally full.*
>
> *The professor went on to explain that the jar signifies one's life.*
>
> *The rocks are equivalent to the most important things in your life. And if the pebbles and the sand were lost, the jar would still be full and your life would still have a meaning.*
>
> *The pebbles represent the other things that matter in your life. These things often come and go, and are not permanent or essential to your overall well-being.*

And finally, the sand represents the remaining small stuff in your life. These things don't mean much to your life as a whole and are likely only done to waste time or get small tasks accomplished.

The metaphor here is that if you start with putting sand into the jar, you will not have room for rocks or pebbles. This holds true for the things you let into your life too.

1. Rocks: Your most important strategic projects
2. Pebbles: Projects and tasks that are important but not the most critical
3. Sand: Smaller, more insignificant tasks

Tackle the rocks first. If you keep tackling the small things (the sand and pebbles), and not the important strategic items, the rocks, then your jar will quickly fill up with no room for more rocks.

Important to make your schedule adjustable

Though you often think you know the priority of your tasks, a new, unexpected task may appear and take first place. Once this happens, you should streamline your to-do list to match your new priorities.

Simply ease out of your current task and focus all your attention on the new task. List it in your planner, so you'll be able to check mark it when done. Make a time estimate for when you might be finished and start working.

Once you're done with this new, important task, resume work on your previous priorities.

"Controlling your time helps overcome frustration and brings life into balance and order, giving you the feeling of control and poise."

— Bill Newman

 **Sole Purpose of Life is to be Happy.**

Happiness Mantra 3 – There is a reason for everything, nothing happens by chance or accident.

Universe has a certain order and everything is bound by a relationship of cause and effect. For every effect, there is a cause.

Remember that, there is reason for everything which happens. Nothing happens by chance or accidently. Whatever is happening to you right now is because you have put certain causes into operation in the past and unless all those causes are gradually worked out in the form of effects and no fresh causes are generated by us, we will not be free and happy for ever.

Based on the above knowledge, change your mental attitude in confronting various incidents and problems of life. Don't view them as burden coming to you out of nowhere. Consider all problems as projects and as means to grow and **remain even minded in success/failure, gain/loss, praise/insult so as to stop any fresh bondage of karma. It is not the incidents or events which are important, but, our mental attitude and reaction towards them.** That is why it has been aptly said that, **"World is neither good nor bad. It depends upon how we look at it?"** Or in other words, it depends on the state of our mind. **Whatever is within us, same appears to us outside.**

Principle of Time Management & Life Management

Parkinson's Law
A bureaucratic evil that we all follow

When students have two or three months to turn in a project, and they end up doing it 24 hours before it is due. Or when you have to complete a work task in the afternoon. You procrastinate up until a couple of hours before the established time.

And during these few hours, you do everything that you hadn't done before?

A bureaucratic evil that we all copy – Parkinson Law.

C. Northcote Parkinson discovered by carefully observed the way that work was carried out in government offices and by observing government employees. Based on his daily experience, he managed to find patterns that allowed him to postulate his basic principles - Parkinson's law, which states,

1. "Work expands so as to fill the time available for its completion."
2. "Expenses will increase until they cover all of the income."
3. "The time dedicated to any topic on the agenda is inversely proportional to its importance."

The time management/productivity hack everyone, who needs to improve his quality of life by managing his time in effective manner, need to know is Parkinson's Law. Parkinson's Law states that work expands to fill the time allotted for its completion.

Time management is all psychological. We naturally pace ourselves to finish a project in the nick of time. The same task can take one hour or one week depending on how much time we give to ourselves to complete it. Ever pull off a big presentation where your only prep was during your commute on the way over? The law is true!

Parkinson's Law has spawned many serviceable corollaries:

1. A wardrobe expands to fill all the available closet space.

Time Management is Life Management

2. A hoarder's corpus of unwanted items and junk expands to fill his available space—in closets, cabinets, attics, garage, etc.
3. Boredom expands to fill the space and time available to an affected individual.
4. Meetings expand to fill the time available. (Appropriately, if you set an hour for the meeting, people will use the entire hour, in spite of how much is on the agenda.)
5. No matter how much money people earn, they tend to spend the entire amount and a little bit more besides.

The main application of Parkinson's Law has been in the administration of time. Its first postulate indicates: "Work expands until it fills the time available for its realization." This means that if you have an hour to perform a task, you are going to take an hour to perform it. But if you have a month, you will take a month to do it.

> *"Time and money never last enough. However, if we look at it closely, this is due to the mistaken way that we administrate them."*

Many of us are guilty of assigning work to ourselves and blocking out time to get the work done. The problem is, we probably block out too much time.

- Half an hour to return phone calls (when the calls we need to make can realistically be done in just a few minutes).
- Two-hour meetings seem to take two-and-a-half hours, but I can often summarize them in two and half minutes to the person who couldn't make it.

These are the two areas I'm guiltiest in practicing Parkinson's Law.

> Years ago — before starting as an advisor & coaching — I spent some time in retail. Busy retail... busy retail with demanding bosses. (Not surprisingly, those were some of the motivating factors for me to turn to entrepreneuring in the first place). In those times, when the mad rush would literally last for 12 hours straight, I learned what could be done in short periods of time: Two-minute phone calls could be made in one minute without sacrificing quality.

Thirty-minute meetings became stand-up, on-the-fly discussions and the proverbial ball was never dropped.

We should all keep Parkinson's law in our minds when we're planning.

This principle is related to another postulate that Parkinson called "The Law of Dilation". He establishes that when you have time, you will always tend to postpone everything you need to do. But, why does this happen? Simply because time is a highly subjective concept. It depends more on our inner perception than the actual passage of hours.

Parkinson also noticed that the more time we dedicate to completing a task, the more complicated it becomes and the more difficult it becomes to complete it. If you have the perception that you have plenty of time at your disposal, you focus more on the details and tend to branch out. You try to cover even the most minimal aspects of the task. Instead, if you are in a hurry, "let's get to the point", without beating around the bush.

Parkinson also noticed that the least important issues were the ones that ended up occupying the biggest amount of time. Hence his third great postulate, "The time dedicated to any topic on the agenda is inversely proportional to its importance."

It seems that relevant issues demand a serious attitude and require precise approaches. That's why they need to be dispatched more efficiently. On the contrary, trivial matters make everyone want to participate and say anything that comes to mind. Therefore, more time is dedicated to them.

Although Parkinson's law was postulated after observing bureaucracy, the truth is it can be applied to practically everyone. And it not only applies to time management. Instead, it also extends to other aspects of life, such as expenses or the organization of physical spaces.

The result of all of these behavioural patterns is a great level of inefficiency.

In order to maximize efficiency at work, check out these productivity hacks that will improve your time management with Parkinson's Law in mind.

Make Deadlines for EVERYTHING

- Don't let any task, no matter how small, have an undefined deadline. Undefined deadlines create undefined game plans. Encourage momentum by tagging everything with a due date. Play a little game, challenge yourself to answer all emails in less than 5 minutes. The next day try to do it in under 3.
- In your calendar, push all deadlines up by a day. Or, take the more adventurous route and move the deadlines up on all your projects, but by different amounts. The psychological nature of Parkinson's law will have to take place because you won't remember when everything is actually due, so you will do them all earlier.

Track Your Time

- How can you maximize your productivity if you don't even know how long you've been working on a task? It's important to regularly monitor your project's work hours. Encourage a daily submission rule for time logs to improve submission accuracy and keep time tracking up-to-date.
- Time tracking encourages you to be hyper-aware of a project's progress. Using data from time tracking, allot 25% less project time to your next project to employ Parkinson's law for maximum efficiency.

Take Breaks

- My personal favorite! Parkinson's Law tells us we can accomplish things in much less time than we think, which is excellent news because our brains work best if we take a small break after 90 minutes of work. Working straight for periods longer than that just leaves us tired and our quality of work goes straight out the door. So yes, let it be known, not doing work actually helps your productivity.
- According to Parkinson's Law, work can contract to fill in the time you give it. You can apply artificial limitations to

your work in order to finish it more efficiently. Consider setting time limits on all your activities.

> Set a timer for each task you're trying to get done. If you reckon something may take 90 minutes, set a timer for 90 minutes—or better yet, challenge yourself to be more efficient by setting a timer for 60 minutes. During that time, allow no interruptions and distractions. Keep your nose to the grindstone, apply yourself thoroughly to the task, and get it done.

For habitual procrastinators who tend to put off looming tasks to a later time and exert themselves at the "last minute" prior to an imminent deadline, one other corollary to Parkinson's Law may be helpful: "If you wait until the last minute, it only takes a minute to do," possibly producing mediocre results.

"All that really belongs to us is time; even he who has nothing else has that."

— Baltasar Gracian

Principle of Time Management & Life Management

Biological Prime Time
Manage your Energy to make Time productive

When students have two or three months to turn in a project, and they end up doing it 24 hours before it is due. Or when you have to complete a work task in the afternoon. You procrastinate up until a couple of hours before the established time.

And during these few hours, you do everything that you hadn't done before?

Understand your biological prime time.

We all have a time of day when we are at our most productive. For most people, this is limited to about three hours, and it comes at different times of day for different people. This is the time when you have the most energy, the time of day when you can really get things done. **This is "Prime Time", and identifying it and protecting it is a critical component of Time Accountability.**

It is really important for you to identify what your "Prime Time" is and then plan your day around it. For some people, it is first thing in the morning; for others it is late at night. In my case, my best time is in the morning, and I try to run my day using my "Prime Time" for things that require creativity so that I maximize my productivity and effectiveness.

It is important to understand your biological prime time. Everyone of us has different biological prime time. That's the time of day when you are at your best. Are you a "morning person", a "night owl", or a late afternoon "whiz"?

> **Knowing when your best time is and planning to use that time of day for your priorities (if possible) is effective time management.**

Your internal prime time is the time of day, according to your body clock, when you are the most alert and productive. For most people, this is in the morning. For some people, however, it is in the evening. Occasionally, a writer, an artist, or an entertainer may find that her prime time is in the early hours of the morning. Listening to your body and identifying your own prime time is essential to achieve all of your goals. If one of your goal is to learn how to write a book, part of your prime time should be dedicated to planning, writing, editing, and marketing your book.

It is important that you be aware of your internal prime time so that you can schedule your most important projects accordingly to increase productivity. Your most important work usually requires that you be at your very best, rested, alert, and creative. What time of the day do you most feel this way?

Having identified your "Prime Time", the first thing you need to do is to plan your day around it. You need to set it aside so that you can use it to work on the most important things in your business life and accomplish the things that can really make a difference. Then you need to figure out how to protect it. It is all too easy to allow routine activities and interruptions to intrude, and you need to be proactive about making sure that this doesn't happen.

It may be that your most productive time of day coincides with the time when you have to interact with customers and prospects, and if that is the time of day when you are at your most creative, it can create a problem. Some of your "Prime Time" may need to be spent in this way, but if you spend all of it selling and reacting, then you will never spend your most productive time on some of the most important things in your business and you are, effectively, being run by "the tyranny of the urgent".

"Prime Time" can potentially yield significantly more value than even your most important sales time. If all your "Prime Time" is used selling and putting out fires, you should take a long hard look at this and perhaps re-evaluate some aspects of your business model.

It all starts with understanding the value of your time.

You must also be aware of external prime time. This is the time when your customers or clients are most readily available. Each person should give some thought to structuring their day for both their external and internal prime times.

While some of us accomplish more work before breakfast than for the rest of the day, others hit their stride after dinner. Peak performance times are deeply personal, and don't always sync with work schedules and life responsibilities.

Once you determine your own prime time for getting things done, there are many ways to take advantage of it and accomplish more.

Biological Prime Time

The phrase was first coined by Sam Carpenter in his book "Work the System" – the gist of this particular time management technique is to identify your most productive hours in the day, and then schedule your days accordingly. A timesheet calculator is a handy tool for this.

Your Biological Prime Time depends on your ultradian rhythms – these are cycles your body goes through each day, and they determine your prime hours during the day. **According to the book and research where the term was coined, people function in cycles of 90-120 minutes.**

> During these cycles, you first feel unproductive, then experience a surge of productivity, before your productivity levels dwindle down again.

Calculate your Biological Prime Time

The key in calculating your Biological Prime Time is tracking your energy levels.

The more days you spend tracking this, the more accurate results you'll get – so, pursue the experiment for 20 days at the least.

Consider your energy levels every hour, of every day – depending on how productive, alert, and focused you feel, write any number from 1-10 next to each hour. So, 1 means extremely low levels, and 10 means extremely high levels.

After you've charted in your energy levels per hour for three weeks, you'll get a clear reading on when you're the most alert.

If you've entered your data in an Excel sheet, you'll be able to create your own line chart, showing how your energy levels rise and fall during the day.

You'll also be able to identify the absolute peak hours for your energy levels – for example, if you usually gave high scores (8, 9 or 10) to 11 am, 2 pm and 6 pm, these are your peaks.

So, it's best that you perform most important work during these times, for maximum productivity – you'll feel energized enough to tackle priorities faster, and in a quality way.

Protect your prime time

Micromanaging your schedule to ensure you don't take on too much makes it more likely your prime time can be focused on priority tasks.

Try to block out many of those peak performance hours on your schedule and consider them sacrosanct and non-negotiable.

Plan ahead for productivity

Productivity experts recommend matching your most difficult tasks to your most productive times.

For many of us, that is first thing in the morning. Importantly, "the first thing you accomplish at work sets the tone for the rest of the day," as per experts. To kickstart your workday with a quick and significant win, Brian Tracy recommends you "eat the frog first" – tackling the most high priority (and perhaps dreaded) task on your desk before getting lost in the busy work of email or being distracted by co-workers.

"When you use your most productive hours you can make a lot of progress, and that progress is motivational."

— **Laura Vanderkam**

Manage microtasks

Keep a list of micro-tasks for those small gaps in your schedule.

You may find your most productive hours change throughout the week or vary from task to task.

What items can you accomplish in transit, or on your phone? Make it a habit to postpone non-critical email responses and use read-it-later apps like Evernote or Pocket, so your phone can be a productivity tool in moments of micro boredom and downtime.

"Always have an article to read for times when you are standing in line, on a bus, or waiting for an event to begin - use all those little bits of time to your advantage."

Time management + energy management

We know time is our most precious and finite resource. Paying closer attention to the choices we make about how to spend it may explain why we find ourselves exhausted at the end of the day, with too many unfinished tasks.

> **"Monitor your working habits for one week and list the time you managed to do the most work,"** Over time, inevitably a pattern will emerge, indicating your peak hours for creative and constructive work.

Win-win: being more productive also means having more downtime.

To shield those precious hours from the time sucks of social media and email, check out and consider installing some social blocking and inbox management apps.

Start the week off right

Don't be surprised if on reflection you find that Monday and Tuesday are your most productive days of the week.

You now know the basics, but here are further points you can consider about your Biological Prime Time findings.

1. During your test period, avoid alcohol, nicotine and caffeine
2. Feeling fully alert at 7 a.m. on a Monday? Well, if you've just had coffee, caffeine might be the main thing holding you together.
3. Feeling drowsy at 8 a.m. on a Tuesday? If you went out for drinks with friends the evening before, you might want to blame it on the alcohol.
4. Staying up every night past 12 a.m.? The cigarettes you smoke in the evenings disrupt your natural sleeping patterns.

As you can see, all three substances disrupt your regular biological patterns. So, unless you give them up for at least the next three weeks, you won't get an accurate reading for your Biological Prime Time.

As often as you can, avoid waking up to an alarm

Letting yourself wake up naturally is the best way to learn about your natural energy patterns, so you should practice this often.

But, as you probably won't be able to sleep in until 9 a.m. every day, no matter how natural it feels (after all, you have to go to work), perhaps it's best that you leave this part of the experiment for holidays and vacation time.

Simply, go to bed when you're tired, and get up when you naturally wake up and feel rested enough.

Use your energy dips wisely

You've found your energy peak times, but that doesn't mean the rest of your day is doomed to be a waste of time.

You can spend your less productive hours tackling less immediate tasks like meetings, going through your emails, business phone or Skype calls Or, you can spend these hours by engaging in any other activity that doesn't require a lot of effort, but is still in your to-do list.

As an alternative, you can make use of your energy dips to meditate, go for a walk, or take part in some other healthy activity.

It is a fact that not all people function in the same manner. Some are more productive at certain times of the day than others. This is where the concepts of "morning person" and "night owls" are considered. It is a matter of identifying the time of the day where your energy levels are high. Most likely, that is also your most productive time, or your "prime time". By assigning the high-priority and complex tasks or the tasks that require a lot of attention during your prime time, you are increasing the probability that these tasks will be completed or accomplished without any problems.

 *The world doesn't reward perfection. It rewards productivity.*

Principle of Time Management & Life Management

Don't let perfection be a curse

They did not want it Perfect, they wanted it on good enough, and on Yesterday

Things may need to be undertaken carefully, thoroughly, comprehensively, but we may not need to spend time getting every tiny detail perfect and fail to deliver work on time.

A good plan violently executed now is better than a perfect plan next week - Post deadline.

Perfectionism is a double-edged sword.

"It has to be perfect!" - Do you ever find yourself saying that?

On one hand, it can motivate you to perform at a high level and deliver top-quality work. On the other hand, it can cause you unnecessary anxiety and slow you down. It is important to understand best way to harness the positives of your perfectionism while mitigating the negatives.

Overcoming perfectionism is essential if you want to know how to manage your time and your life. It's about adopting an attitude and forming a habit that will serve rather than control you. Perfectionism is a learned mindset that causes stress.

It's easy to get caught up trying to make something better than it really needs to be, but it takes its toll. Time, effort and energy are spent that could, and probably should, be deployed elsewhere.

One of the important principles of effective time management is to know when it's time to stop.

Whether it's a project, task or even (especially) something that distracts you, improve your ability to know when enough is enough and you're on the way to overcoming perfectionism.

Time Management is Life Management

 It may surprise you to know that people with perfectionist tendencies actually tend to struggle with effective use of their time.

Ready-Fire-Aim

- ➢ Apart from being a helpful mindset for overcoming procrastination, 'ready-fire-aim' means plan it, do it, then adjust it.
- ➢ Don't wait for everything to be just right before you release it to the world. Adequate planning is important, but actually producing something is what matters.
- ➢ Get it out there, then refine it. Tweak it, polish it and make it better, but remember that, in this context, the most effective use of your time is to know when to stop planning and actually do something.

Embrace your mistakes

Overcoming perfectionism means embracing mistakes, taking criticism and accepting 'failure' will inevitably sometimes be the result. In short, we're all human, and we all get things wrong.

Mistakes, criticism and not achieving what we want are always hard. They can be frustrating and demoralizing, but they can also be some of the most valuable lessons. If you're prepared to learn from them, you'll get better at whatever matters to you.

Next time you find yourself hampered by 'perfection paralysis', remind yourself that it's better to do and say sorry than to do and say nothing.

 If you're not grading diamonds or building nuclear weapons, you might want to ease up on the perfectionism.

Don't produce perfection – aim to produce perfectly

Instead of striving for perfection in whatever you do, concentrate on getting better at estimating how much time and effort to put into anything and everything you produce.

Time Management is Life Management

Aim to be perfect, not at what you do, but how you do it. This sounds contradictory, but it's actually about fitting your role, goal or task to the time, situation and circumstances you're in.

The better you get at that, the more effectively you use your time in relation to what you choose to do. If something deserves several hours of concentrated energy and, on reflection, you didn't put the time in, ask yourself why, and learn from it. Similarly, if you spent too long on something that didn't really need that much attention, accept it as a lesson, learn from your experience and give it the attention it deserves next time.

Dealing with perfectionism starts with small steps. Gradually shift your mindset from 'producing perfect' to 'producing perfectly' and you'll start to work the Pareto Principle to your advantage.

None of us would certainly not advocate that anyone adopts a shoddy approach to their work, whatever it may be. There is, however, a well summed up famous quotation from Robert Heimleur, who said (perhaps despairingly): "They didn't want it good, they wanted it on Wednesday."

Not denying to the fact is it takes time to achieve perfection, and in any case perfection may not always be strictly necessary. Things may need to be undertaken carefully, thoroughly, comprehensively, but we may not need to spend time getting every tiny detail perfect.

This comes hard to those who are naturally perfectionists time style owner, and it is a trait that many people have, at least about some things.

It is necessary to strike a balance. There is always a trade-off here, and it is not always the easiest thing to achieve. Often a real compromise has to be made. You have to make decisions about how to do things based on quality, cost, . . . and time.

1. Cost is often crucial in this. It would be easy to achieve the quality of output you want in many things, but only if cost were no object. And, in most jobs budget considerations rank high. It is useful to get into the way of thinking about things in these terms, and doing so realistically so that you consider what is necessary as well as (or instead of?) what is simply desirable or ideal. In doing this, there is

one key factor that needs to be built in: the significant, and sometimes the largest, cost of your time.
2. Consider all the costs of your working on something; the resultant figure may surprise you. Let me repeat: make sure by all means that what must be done to perfection is done in a way that achieves just that. Otherwise make sure you always keep in mind the balance to be struck among quality, cost, and time; if you do not over-engineer quality, seeking a standard that is not in some instances necessary or desirable, then you will surely save time.

Experts today describes perfectionists as people who "often get hung up on meaningless details and spend more time on projects than is necessary." The end result of this single-minded focus: reduced productivity, stress, and waste of time.

Wanting to do your best is an admirable quality, and there are some situations (of the life-or-death variety) where cutting corners is not an option. But if you are wasting time and resources by attempting to achieve perfection in your day-to-day tasks, then you are hindering the productivity of your team by creating a bottleneck & time management problem. While having high standards is paramount to success, having unrealistic expectations of yourself and your co-workers can negatively impact your relationships, your self-esteem, and your career.

Traits of a perfectionist

1. Does every project — no matter how big or small — get equal attention and treated with the same sense of urgency?
2. Are you frequently stymied by analysis paralysis, using much of your project's time to weigh many options before taking action?
3. Do you often feel frustrated that you don't have enough time to finish your work?

Other tell-tale signs:
- Focusing on the outcome, not the journey
- Noticing the small imperfections in your work and others', rather than the overall result

- Not wanting to participate in something that you do not excel at
- Difficulty delegating tasks to others for fear they might not be done correctly

As perfectionists are often hindered by self-doubt or exceptionally high standards, they miss deadlines. Using following steps, you can keep your work on track, and your organization's goals in focus:

1. Despite your instincts, assign an urgency and a priority to each task. All tasks are not created equal. It's in your DNA to put forth your best effort for every project. But not all projects require the same level of intensity.
2. Get a second opinion. If you're not sure how to prioritize your projects, ask your team lead or manager. Everything may feel like it's a high-value project, but there could be some items that need to move ahead of others on your to-do list.

Get started. **A close cousin to perfectionism is procrastination.** If you feel like you can't start a project until you have the perfect solution, just dive in anyway. Wanting to get things right is admirable, but not when it's done at the expense of deadlines. If it happens often enough, it can damage your reputation, and potentially your job security. So even if you don't have all the details to start on a project, start on whatever component you can start on while you wait for the missing info to trickle in.

- Bottom Line – Set limits. If you have a tendency to work and re-work a task past its deadline, set a time limit for yourself. Timers can be effective tools for managing time spent on a project. When the timer goes off, move on to something else. And when the deadline is approaching, hand your work off to someone else for a quick run-through to get another perspective on its quality.
- Be realistic. Everything can't be perfect. Don't give up, though! Nobody likes to make mistakes, but just because something can't be the very best doesn't mean it's not worth doing.

➢ Remember the big picture. If you're having trouble wrapping up a project because it's not quite perfect yet, ask yourself: How will additional work affect the outcome? Will the end result be vastly improved? Will the project be late? If your perfectionism is ultimately hurting rather than helping the project, you'll need to adjust your behavior.

There's nothing wrong with wanting to do a good job. They key is knowing when "good" is "good enough". You must learn to balance your own expectations of your work with the expectations of your leadership team. Save perfection for the projects where it's going to be valued by all involved.

Identifying those behaviors that hamper your output is a solid first step in understanding how they impact your work, life, and personal relationships. Being self-aware and open to adjusting your thought processes makes it easier for you to improve your time management skills, thereby improving your productivity.

"One worthwhile task carried to a successful conclusion is worth half-a-hundred half-finished tasks."

— **Malcolm S. Forbes**

 13		Principle of Time Management & Life Management
		Procrast-I-nation –
		Nationwide problem
		We all are natural Procrastinator

 *"In a moment of decision, the best thing you can do is the right thing to do, the next best thing is the wrong thing, and the worst thing you can do is nothing."*

— **Theodore Roosevelt**

Procrastination is natural human tendency.

Do any of the following descriptions apply to you?

1. My paper is due in three days and I haven't really started writing it yet.
2. I've had to pull an all-nighter to get an assignment done on time.
3. I've turned in an assignment late or asked for an extension when I really didn't have a good excuse not to get it done on time.
4. I've worked right up to the minute an assignment was due.
5. I've underestimated how long a reading assignment would take and didn't finish it in time for class.
6. I've relied on the Internet for information (like a summary of a concept or a book) because I didn't finish the reading on time.

If these sound like issues you've struggled with in the past, you might want to consider whether you have the tendency to procrastinate and how you want to deal with it in your future classes. You're already spending a lot of time, energy, and money on the classes you're taking—don't let all of that go to waste!

> **Procrastination is a way of thinking that lets one put off doing something that should be done now.**

We all procrastinate to some extent. The result is that high-priority tasks are postponed or, worse, never completed, making the procrastinators feel guilty. There are generally three reasons for procrastination:

1. Unpleasant and Uninteresting Tasks

Sandra knows that she must confront Helen, her subordinate, about Helen's habit of getting to work late every day, but she has done nothing to address the problem. In this case, Sandra's procrastination is an unconscious way of avoiding an unpleasant task: personal confrontation. The same avoidance happens with uninteresting tasks. Here are some cures for this form of procrastination:

Tasks that are unpleasant to you might not be unpleasant to someone else, so delegate them if possible.

If you cannot delegate, look at the situation objectively and admit that you're procrastinating because you find the task unpleasant. Think about the relief you'll feel after you've addressed the unpleasant task.

Schedule the unpleasant task in a way that will make it difficult or impossible to turn back. In the above example, Sandra can email and schedule a meeting with Helen.

2. Fear of Failure

We all are naturally tempted to avoid a task that may lead to failure. In most cases the best way to handle fear is to confront it directly. If you fear that you lack the training or resources to successfully complete an assignment, then get the help you need. If your fear from a lack of self-confidence, defuse that fear through planning all the things required to successfully complete the job.

3. Not Knowing Where to Begin

The lack of clarity in some jobs encourages procrastination. Two remedies for this type of situation are:

- ➢ Jump in anywhere. After you're in the game, it's likely that you will find a productive way forward, reducing any inclination to procrastinate.

Time Management is Life Management   107

> Break the job into its component parts and tasks necessary to complete each part. Arrange these in a logical sequence, and begin with the first task as you move forward.

This can happen to anyone at any time. It's like a voice inside your head keeps coming up with these brilliant ideas for things to do right now other than studying: "I really ought to get this room cleaned up before I study" or "I can study anytime, but tonight's the only chance I have to do X." That voice is also very good at rationalizing: "I really don't need to read that chapter now; I'll have plenty of time tomorrow at lunch...."

Combat Procrastination - Overcome Procrastination Using the **4D System**

1. *Delete it:* What are the consequences of not doing the task at all? Consider the 80/20 rule; maybe it doesn't need to be done in the first place.
2. *Delegate it:* If the task is important, ask yourself if it's really something that you are responsible for doing in the first place. Can the task be given to someone else?
3. *Do it now:* Postponing an important task that needs to be done only creates feelings of anxiety and stress. Do it as early in the day as you can.
4. *Defer:* If the task is one that can't be completed quickly and is not a high priority item, simply defer it.

David Allen's "Getting Things Done: The Art of Stress-Free Productivity" has a wonderful methodology. He calls it the "2-Minute Rule" and it's a great way to beat procrastination and get things done. It works for both your professional and personal life.

There are two parts to the "2-Minute Rule":

Part 1: If it can be done in two minutes, just do it. Don't add it to your to-do list, put it aside for later, or delegate to someone else. Just do it.

Here are some examples of tasks you can do in two minutes or less:

> Answer an email from your boss
> Send an update to a colleague

- Make a plan for the day while having your morning coffee
- Loading the dishwasher right after the meal
- There are a ton of tiny, seemingly trivial tasks that take less than two minutes yet you need to do every day.

Part 2: If it takes more than two minutes, start it. Once you start acting on small tasks, you can keep the ball rolling. Simply working on it for two minutes will help you break the first barrier of procrastination.

- Write a thousand words every day? Write 50 words in the next two minutes
- Meditate for 20 minutes a day? Sit down and meditate for two minutes
- Want to exercise for one hour a day? Do jumping jacks for just two minutes
- 9 out of 10 times I end up working on the task for far longer than 2 minutes (Post this, you can continue working using the Pomodoro productivity method).
- Procrastination is very powerful. Some people battle it daily, others only occasionally. Most college students procrastinate often, and about half say they need help to avoid procrastination. Procrastination can threaten one's ability to do well on an assignment or test.
- People procrastinate for different reasons. Some people are too relaxed in their priorities, seldom worry, and easily put off responsibilities. Others worry constantly, and that stress keeps them from focusing on the task at hand. Some procrastinate because they fear failure; others procrastinate because they fear success or are so perfectionistic that they don't want to let themselves down. Some are dreamers. Many different factors are involved, and there are different styles of procrastinating.

Just as there are different causes, there are different possible solutions for procrastination. Different strategies work for different people. Procrastination is a psychological issue, some additional psychological strategies can also help:

- Since procrastination is usually a habit, accept that and work on breaking it as you would any other bad habit: one day at a time. Know that every time you overcome feelings of procrastination, the habit becomes weaker and eventually, you'll have a new habit of being able to start studying right away.
- Schedule times for studying using a daily or weekly planner. Commit to your study schedule in the same way you commit to other obligations like class time or school. Carry it with you and look at it often. Just being aware of the time and what you need to do today can help you get organized and stay on track.
- If you keep thinking of something else you might forget to do later (making you feel like you "must" do it now), write yourself a note about it for later and get it out of your mind.
- Counter a negative with a positive. If you're procrastinating because you're not looking forward to a certain task, try to think of the positive future results of doing the work, like getting a good grade or raising your GPA.
- Counter a negative with a worse negative. If thinking about the positive results of completing the task doesn't motivate you to get started, think about what could happen if you keep procrastinating. You'll have to study tomorrow instead of doing something fun you had planned. Or you could fail the test. Some people can jolt themselves right out of procrastination.

On the other hand, fear causes procrastination in some people—so don't dwell on the thought of failing. If you're studying for a test, and you're so afraid of failing it that you can't focus on studying and you start procrastinating, try to put things in perspective. Even if it's your most difficult class and you don't understand everything about the topic, that doesn't mean you'll fail, even if you may not receive an A or a B.

- Study with a motivated friend. Form a study group with other students who are motivated and won't procrastinate along with you. You'll learn good habits from them while getting the work done now.

- Keep your studying "bite-sized": When confronted with 150 pages of reading or 50 problems to solve, it's natural to feel overwhelmed. Try breaking it down: What if you decide that you will read for 45 minutes or that you will solve 10 problems? That sounds much more manageable.
- Turn off your phone, close your chat windows, and block distracting Web sites. Treat your studying as if you're in a movie theater—just turn it off.
- Set up a reward system: If you read for 40 minutes, you can check your phone for 5 minutes. But keep in mind that reward-based systems only work if you stick to an honor system.
- Study in a place reserved for studying ONLY. Your bedroom may have too many distractions (or temptations, such as taking a nap), so it may be best to avoid it when you're working on school assignments.
- Use checklists: Make your incremental accomplishments visible. Some people take great satisfaction and motivation from checking items off a to-do list. Be very specific when creating this list, and clearly describe each task one step at a time.
- Get help. If you really can't stay on track with your study schedule, or if you're always putting things off until the last minute, see a college counselor. They have lots of experience with this common student problem and can help you find ways to overcome this habit.

"You may delay, but time will not, and lost time is never found again."

— **Benjamin Franklin**

		Principle of Time Management & Life Management
		# Learn to Say No Many a times, No is better than Yes

"Let today mark a new beginning for you. Give yourself permission to say NO without feeling guilty, mean, or selfish. Anybody who gets upset or expects you to say yes all of the time clearly doesn't have your best interest at heart. Always remember: You have a right to say no without having to explain yourself. Be at peace with your decisions."

— **Stephanie Lahartcan**

When you say No, you are only saying No to one option.
When you say Yes, you are saying No to every other option.
No is a decision.
Yes is a responsibility.
Be careful when (and who) you say Yes to. It will shape your day, your career, your family, your life.

 *"When you say 'yes' to others, make sure you are not saying 'no' to yourself."*

— **Paulo Coelho**

Half of the troubles of this life can be traced to saying YES too quickly and not saying NO soon enough.

Strangely, the capacity to say no is firmly connected to fearlessness. Individuals with low self-assurance and confidence regularly feel anxious about irritating others and tend to rate others' needs more exceptionally than their own.

Warren Buffet said it best: "The difference between successful people and very successful people is that very successful people say no to almost everything."

But, how do you know which things you should say no to? What if you are passing on a life-changing opportunity? Luckily,

Buffet has developed a two-step rule to help you set boundaries and become better at decision making:
- ➢ Start by writing down your top twenty-five career goals. Once you're done, circle the five most important to you
- ➢ The second step is to completely eliminate the other twenty goals. Go ahead and cross them off

Say "no" by default to anything that doesn't contribute to your top 5 career goals.

Anything other than the five goals you circled in the first step are distractions getting in the way of reaching what you truly value in life. As such, start saying no to anything that doesn't contribute to your "true goals".

An ability to say "No" is not only a sign of self-confidence and assertiveness, but is crucial to our ability to effectively manage our time. Those with time management issues often say "Yes" too much, impacting their overall productivity and performance. Here, we look at how you can improve your time management and efficiency by learning to say "No" more often.

Understand the implications of saying Yes

Agreeing to something in the workplace usually means making a commitment and taking on additional responsibility. You will be committing time, resources and action, which will inevitably affect your workload and impact your ability to manage your time effectively.

Understanding how saying "Yes" will impact your carefully planned schedule is critical to know when you really can't afford to answer in the affirmative.

Listen carefully and ask questions

When someone comes to you with a request, make sure you listen carefully to what they are asking of you. If you are unsure, ask questions, as simple-sounding requests can often lead to much more time and resources than you might imagine.

Before you give your response, make sure you understand the implications, important and requirements of what is being asked.

Give reasons for saying No

If you do have to decline a request, it will almost certainly be received more positively if you can give a reason, rather than simply saying no.

Whether it is existing commitments to another colleague or project, a schedule clash, a lack of appropriate resources or any other reason, try to demonstrate that you have given their request genuine consideration and not just decline immediately.

Avoid an instant answer

Whenever someone makes a new request, be sure to take the time to consider their request carefully. Pausing will give you the time to weigh up how it will affect your workflow allowing you to understand the implications of saying yes.

Only agree to take something on if you can fully commit to it, meaning it is not going to negatively impact your productivity and profitability, and you can adhere to your own quality standards.

Strategy to Effectively Saying "No"

1. Buy Yourself Some Time

Be sure to buy yourself some time when someone makes a new request. Point out that you need to check your schedule or current workload and suggest you come back to them in a specified period. Not only will this make it easier to say no, but it will demonstrate that you have given their request genuine consideration.

2. Offer Alternative Solutions

You will almost certainly find it easier to say no if you can offer an alternative solution, particularly if the request comes from a superior.

This might mean suggesting another person to help, agreeing to assist in the future or delegating to team members, and you will likely find you get a positive response even though you are saying No.

3. Use "Not Right Now"

Rather than simply saying "No" to a request, you might find people reach better to "not right now". This is particularly useful if it is a project or task you are interested in or qualified to help with, but your short-term schedule is too busy to deal with right away. This also shows that you take your current responsibilities seriously, and that you are only willing to commit when you can give your full attention.

Too many times we get badgered until we finally say yes. Unfortunately, too many people can't or won't take no for an answer so they continue to ask until you agree. This is probably because too many people use other words that give the person hope that you'll say yes:

- Maybe
- Let me think about it
- I'll get back with you
- I need to check my calendar
- We'll see.

We all wrestle such time management issue. When I'm asked to attend a meeting, go to lunch, take in a move, etc., and I don't want to or can't, to respond this way:

I appreciate you thinking of me, but I cannot.

You don't owe an explanation, and after you've used this technique consistently, people will realize you mean what you say. In the meantime, you might be pressed to change your mind. Your response can be:

I respect the fact that you want me to attend; please respect the fact that I cannot.

Other responses, depending on the request, are kind but firm:

- I'm honored that you invited me; however, I must decline.
- I would love to, but my schedule does not permit another item on my calendar.
- This sounds like a great opportunity, but at this time my family needs my attention.
- Your request is tempting, but when I agree to do something I give it 100%. At this time, I know I would not be able to do that, so rather than disappoint you and myself, I must pass.

These simple statements allow you take your life back and politely, but firmly, say no.

Remember, saying no is not selfish. Saying no is not rude. Saying no is not wrong.

Saying no to others is saying yes to yourself. Then, when something comes along that you do want to do, you'll have the time to graciously, and happily, accept.

"One key to successful relationships is learning to say no without guilt, so that you can say yes without resentment."

— **Bill Crawfordagain**

Sole Purpose of Life is to be Happy.

Happiness Mantra 4 – Overcome Fears

Universe by the Law of Attraction, whatever we fear or doubt, we actually attract those conditions and circumstances around us, and so we are further trapped in a vicious circle.

Fears are a drain on our mental energy and are main stumbling blocks to our progress. There are some people among us who constantly fear lest this or that should happen and thus keep their minds constant in a state of agitation and turmoil.

Please remember, there is nothing in this world which we really need to fear. **Nothing is designed in the Universe to harm us.** One of the best ways to remove fears is to intentionally face and stand before those very things you fear denying mentally that they can do any harm to you, till such time when the fear is totally gone. The causes of your fear leap on you again and again until you overcome fear. It is a law that the more you fear a thing, the more it frightens you. However, if you don't fear and stand before it untouched and indifferent, the opposite happens i.e. the fear will go away from you. Also bear in mind this great truth that actual mishappening is never that fearful and painful as our thought or imagination of that happening.

Even incidents of so called ghosts, black magic, soul possession and various other para-psychical influences affect only those persons who are mentally fearful, weak and remain sensitive to these things. These things can't touch a strong-minded person.

Further, also gain strength by the knowledge that nothing happens by chance or by accident. For every happening, there is a reason. Hence, why the fear of anything suddenly happening to you. Just face each challenge of life boldly with positive outlook and firm faith in God who only can provide the real security to us.

	 Principle of Time Management & Life Management **Start Your Day with MIT** MIT – Most Important Task

 *"Mark Twain once said: "If it's your job to eat a frog, it's best to do it first thing in the morning. And If it's your job to eat two frogs, it's best to eat the biggest one first."*

— **Mark Twain**

When you start your workday, what's the first task you do? How do you decide?

Do you make a conscious choice, or do you jump into whatever feels most urgent? (For too many people, this is automatically processing their email.)

Here's something simple I've learned:

Do your most important task first.

That seems simple enough, and you've likely heard this before. But let's dig into the real question here...

What is your most important task (MIT)?

To determine this, you have to weigh three things:

1. Impact
2. Urgency
3. Your energy/motivation

1. Tasks based on impact produce major results and future influence. The highest impact tasks are multipliers – the work put in now creates a multiplier effect in the future, as opposed to a single result.

The simplest example would be training someone who will have increasingly higher output in the future. This doesn't save us time now…in fact it has the opposite effect. However, it will save us time and mental space in the future. The person will go on to produce much more than we ever could on our own.

Other examples are expanding your expertise through self-development, planning projects, relationship building, or doing work that has highly consequential output (like a major presentation or a published piece of work to a large audience). These tasks are all highly important but are often NOT highly urgent – so this is the best time to do them. If you wait until they become urgent, you'll rush the work and won't optimize the results.

Impact tasks done well now save you time and stress later.

2. Tasks based on urgency are the ones that can't wait a day longer. If you have those, do those first.

But beware of which tasks actually can't wait a day longer versus which tasks you feel can't wait a day longer. A good way to gauge this is by asking this question:

If I suddenly started to feel ill, would I need to get this task done before checking out for the day?

These tasks are critical because of unmovable timelines or because others depend on you. Ideally these tasks are completed as impact tasks, before they become urgent. As you get better at prioritizing impact tasks, your frequency of doing urgent tasks will decline significantly.

3. Tasks based on your energy and motivation prioritizes tasks based on knowing your rhythms throughout the day. You'll be less resistant to doing certain tasks if you figure out when you can best tackle them. We differ in our peaks and troughs, so how you order your tasks versus how I would order the same tasks may be different.

Personally, I am most focused when I start my day. As the day goes on, I often fatigue and lose focus. This seems to be the case for most people I've talked to about work habits. But not everyone. Some people find they are most focused after lunch or even in the evening. Either way, understanding when you are most focused can help you better schedule your tasks.

When deciding which task to do first, you'll need to weigh all three factors of impact, urgency and energy. I will often prioritize doing a low impact task that I dislike doing over a high impact task. I'd prefer to do my high-impact task in the morning, but I know that if I leave my disliked task until later in the day, it usually doesn't get done well, or doesn't get done at all. I'll only do this though, if I know I'll be excited and motivated enough to do the high impact task later in the day.

Know what's important, what's truly urgent, and what your rhythms are.

Then plan and execute on your most important tasks.

Start the Day with Critical Work

This is a golden time management technique: Find your most important task (MIT) for the day and tackle it first. Your MIT should be the one thing that creates the most impact on your work. Getting it done will give you the momentum and sense of accomplishment early in the day. That's how big life goals are achieved: small continuous efforts, day after day.

Each day, identify the most crucial tasks to complete and tackle it first. Once you're done, the day has already been a success!

How do you find your MIT

In Elon Musk's words: "Focus on signal over noise. Don't waste time on stuff that doesn't actually make things better." Look at your to-do list and decide which tasks help you get close to your goals and make progress in meaningful work.

Put these at the top of your list so you can focus on them first. Resist the temptation of tackling the easiest tasks first.

Productivity, Simplified

No need to draw this out. This productivity tip is straightforward: *Do the most important thing first each day.*

Sounds simple. No one does it.

Why It Works

We often assume that **productivity means getting more things done each day.**

Wrong.

Productivity is getting important things done consistently. And no matter what you are working on, there are only a few things that are truly important.

Being productive is about maintaining a steady, average speed on a few things, not maximum speed on everything. That's why this strategy is effective. If you do the most important thing first each day, then you'll always get something important done. I don't know about you, but this is a big deal for me. There are many days when I waste hours crossing off the 4th, 5th, or 6th most important tasks on my to-do list and never get around to doing the most important thing.

As you'll see below, there is no reason you have to apply this strategy in the morning, but I think starting your day with the most important task does offer some additional benefits over other times.

First, **willpower tends to be higher earlier in the day.** That means you'll be able to provide your best energy and effort to your most important task.

Second, in my experience, the deeper I get into the day, the more likely it is that unexpected tasks will creep into my schedule and the less likely it is that I'll spend my time as I had planned. Doing the most important thing first each day helps avoid that.

Finally, the human mind seems to dislike unfinished projects. They create an unresolved tension and internal stress. When we start something, we want to finish it. You are more likely to finish a task after starting it, so start the important tasks as soon as possible. (Just another reason why getting started is more important than succeeding.)

Why We Don't Do It

Most people spend most of their time responding to someone else's agenda than their own.

I think this is partially a result of how we are raised by society. In school, we are given assignments and told when to take our tests. At work, we are assigned due dates and given expectations from our superiors. At home, we have tasks or chores to perform to care for our kids and our partners. After a few decades of this, it can become very easy to spend your day reacting to the stimuli that surround you. We learn to take action as a reaction to the expectations, orders, or needs of someone else.

So naturally, when it comes time to start our day, it doesn't seem strange to open our email inbox, check our phone, and look for our latest marching orders.

I think this is a mistake. The tasks assigned to us by others might seem urgent, but what is urgent is seldom important. The important tasks in our lives are the ones that move our hopes, our dreams, our creations, and our businesses forward.

Does that mean that we should ignore our responsibilities as parents or employees or citizens? Of course not. But we all need a time and space in our days to respond to our own agenda, not someone else's.

Not a Morning Person?

Does the word morning make you mourn? Does the morning sun remind you of The Eye of Sauron? Can you think of nothing worse than rays of golden sunshine streaming softly onto your pillow?

No worries, night owls.

As I scanned the daily habits of hundreds of authors, artists, and musicians in Daily Rituals (audiobook), I noticed an important trend: There was no trend.

There is no one way to be successful. There are just as many night owls producing fabulous work as there are early birds. But no matter what their particular routine looked like, every productive artist embraced the idea of protecting a sacred time each day when they could work on their own agenda.

I find morning to work best. Your mileage may vary.

The phrase "Do the most important thing first each day" is just a simple way of saying, "Give yourself a time and space to work on what is important to you each day."

If you want more practical ideas for breaking bad habits and creating good habits, you need to refer wonderful book Atomic

Habits, which will show you how small changes in habits can lead to remarkable results. I have been immensely benefitted from it.

 *"You've got to think about the big things while you're doing small things, so that all the small things go in the right direction."*

— **Alvin Toffler**

		Principle of Time Management & Life Management
 **16**		# When being "helpful" is actually hurting Say "No" and Delegate or Outsource

In most urgent cases, "If something can be done 80% as well by someone else, delegate or Outsource!"

This is common mistake done by most people as they neither delegate not outsource.

Delegation begins by identifying tasks that others can do and selecting the appropriate person(s) to do them.

Unfortunately, studies show that most knowledge workers spend 41% of their time on tasks they could easily pass off to others. Everybody has their limits. We simply cannot do everything people want us to. It will lead to burnout and work anxiety. That's why it's so important to be assertive and say "no" when people want to assign you additional tasks. Remember, there is nothing wrong with refusing to do things you're not able to do. As well as with delegating tasks. Especially if there is someone, who can do the work better than you. The issue is that while we're aware we could hand off work, the thought of training someone to do it is daunting.

> *Lions cannot afford to hunt mice because they literally will starve to death, even if they catch them. Lions and all large carnivores have to hunt game large enough to justify the investment, so they have to hunt antelope and zebra. Why is this important? Because most senior executives are really big on chipmunks."- Newt Gingrich*

Using the Eisenhower Matrix, you'll find that some tasks are urgent but not important. When that's the case, the best you can do is find someone who can complete these tasks for you. You don't have to do everything yourself. Delegating or outsourcing some tasks can be a great way to multiply your efforts and get more done.

If you work on your own, you can find and hire freelancers. In a team, re-assign specific tasks to colleagues who are better suited to complete specific tasks. Delegate or outsource urgent but not important tasks to multiply yourself and keep you focused on the most important work.

Delegation means assigning responsibility for a task to someone else, freeing up some of your time for tasks that require your expertise. Delegation begins by identifying tasks that others can do and then selecting the appropriate person(s) to do them. You need to select someone with the appropriate skills, experience, interest, and authority needed to accomplish the task.

Be as specific as possible in defining the task and your expectations, but allow the person some freedom to personalize the task. Occasionally check to determine how well the person is progressing and to provide any assistance, being careful not to take over the responsibility. Finally, don't forget to reward the person for a job well done or make suggestions for improvements if needed.

Another way to get help is to "buy" time by obtaining goods or service that save you a time investment. For example, paying someone to mow your lawn or clean your house, using a computerized system, or joining a carpool to transport your children to their extracurricular activities can allow you free time to devote to other activities.

Here are the top things you need to know to delegate efficiently:

1. **Find to the right person:** whoever you're delegating the tasks to should have all the necessary skills and is capable of doing the job

    Provide clear instructions: write down the tasks in a step-by-step manual be as specific as possible

2. **Define success:** be specific about what the expected outcome is and the deadline to have the task completed

3. **Clarity:** have the tasks explained back to you and offer clarification when something is unclear, rewriting the specifications if needed

Why Delegated Tasks Don't Get Done

Delegating is a risk. Something may go wrong and, what is more, as the manager, you may be blamed. So, despite the fact that the risk can be minimized, there is temptation to hang on to things. This makes for two problems: you have too much to do (particularly too many routine tasks) and this keeps you from giving due attention to things that are clear priorities. And staff members do not like it, so motivation—and productivity on the things they are doing—will also be adversely affected. An additional fear is not that the other person will not be able to cope, but that they will cope too well—being better than you. But this is not a reason that should put you off delegating—the potential rewards are too great. Besides, people are more likely to do things differently and that can help development of both individuals and methods.

Key reasons why tasks those have been delegated do not get done (or done right), are -

The employee does not:

➢ understand the task;

➢ have the skills to complete the task;

➢ have the tools or resources needed;

➢ understand why the task need to be done;

➢ know how to deal with an obstacle;

➢ think the task is important; or

➢ want to complete the task.

It is interesting that how many of those reasons could be precluded or mitigated by better two-way communication about the task.

Ten key tips for Delegating Effectively

1. Involve your direct reports in deciding what to delegate.

Allow them to participate in determining what and when tasks are delegated to them, and then get acknowledgement that they understand and agree to the assignment.

2. Communicate expectations clearly and completely.

Be specific, clear, and complete in clarifying the tasks, the goals, resources, constraints, what good performance looks like, and when and how the results will be shared with you.

3. Balance your involvement.

Don't disappear, but don't over-supervise. Hovering is counter-productive. Agree in advance how often you will be updated and under what conditions you need to be informed of issues that arise. Don't swoop in unexpectedly.

4. Push decision-making and authority to the edges of the organization.

Delegate to the lowest level at which the task can be successfully accomplished. Do not bypass your direct report, but encourage him or her to delegate the task when appropriate.

5. Grant authority.

Grant enough authority to do the job, enough power and control over resources to get the job done. Make sure that everyone who is involved knows that you have delegated the authority to your direct report.

6. Provide resources.

Provide all information that is available and relevant; pass on other information as it becomes available. Ensure they have access to the resources needed to be effective.

7. Give credit, withhold blame.

Give public credit when they succeed. If something goes wrong, withhold blame so they don't becoming defensive, and instead help them debrief mistakes and learn from them.

8. Don't take it back.

Require them to first propose their own ideas for solutions when they come to you with a problem. When they ask you for the answer, it is tempting to take on their work. If they have the skills but are lacking confidence or motivation, coach them. Don't take it back unless it is absolutely clear that the situation has become too complex.

9. Maintain accountability.

Although your direct report has the responsibility for seeing the job well done and the authority to make needed decisions, remember that the ultimate accountability remains with you.

10. Delegate consistently.

Delegate consistently, not just when you are overloaded or when tasks are unpleasant.

Achievement through successful delegation, besides Time Management

- It creates opportunity for development and accelerated experience for those to whom matters are delegated.
- It builds morale (precisely because of the opportunity noted above) through the motivational effect of greater job satisfaction, and achievement long and short term in the job (and ultimately beyond it).
- It has broader motivational effects around a team, as well as on the individual.

In addition, there are advantages to you. As a result of the time freed up:

- Time and effort can be concentrated on those aspects of your job that are key to the achievement of objectives.
- A more considered, or creative, approach can be brought to bear, uncluttered by matters that may distract or prevent a broad-brush or longer-term perspective.

Outsource Intelligently

A good rule of thumb for outsourcing is that anything that isn't related to your core competency should be outsourced. Unless you can absolutely justify a full-time resource for a specific function, it's best to outsource to experts that focus on a specific discipline full-time, stay current with the skills and technologies needed, and love to do the work. If you don't have employees to whom you can delegate, outsourcing is a great way to clear your plate of everything you shouldn't be doing. Especially in today's online, platform-centric environment, where everything moves quickly, business owners must turn to specialized experts to keep up.

Basically, any functions that you absolutely must have to run your business but are not related to your competency are great candidates for outsourcing. Your time is best used building your strategy, meeting with prospects, building relationships with your employees and customers, developing your skills that align with your core competency, and establishing yourself as a leading authority in your industry.

Choose Carefully

There is no shortage of seemingly reputable companies to manage your critical tasks. The contingent/outsource workforce continues to grow rapidly. While these trends provide more choices, they also provide more opportunity for mediocrity or problematic work. If you choose to outsource, be selective. Check references, start slowly with a small project, and stay engaged until your partner has proven themselves. Ensure you have a termination clause that releases you from an unsuccessful engagement.

Clearing the tasks that you consider "necessary evils" from your calendar will not only free up your valuable time, it will produce better results, and make you a happier person. Isn't that worth the time it takes to delegate and outsource? Good luck!

"Leaders who are strongest at delegation are those who are dedicated to using the tasks that come across their desks as development opportunities for others."

— **Clemson Turregano**

Principle of Time Management & Life Management
When Manage your Attention, Time will be managed
Say "No" and Delegate or Outsource

A few years ago during a break in a leadership class I was teaching, a manager named Rahul walked up looking unsettled. His boss had told him he needed to be more productive, so he had spent a few hours analyzing how he spent his time. He had already cut his nonessential meetings. He couldn't find any tasks to drop from his calendar. He didn't see an obvious way to do them more efficiently.

He confessed. "My only idea is to drink less water so I don't have to go to the bathroom so many times."

If you want to perform at your best you first need to manage your energy and then your time. Managing your time is managing your attention. - Guy Bieber

It is quoted that Attention span is hardly 7 second when we look at someone else, or hardly 12 minutes when we do our work. In today's time and patience fatigue world, it is decreasing very fast.

"What information consumes is rather obvious. It consumes the attention of its recipients. Hence a wealth of information creates a poverty of attention."

Our attention span is decreasing. As per study conducted by Microsoft, In 200 the average person could focus on one task without being distracted for 12 seconds. In next 15 years, that number has decreased to 8 seconds.

Another problem in our work culture is the fact that we are constantly being interrupted.

Seems like every minute there is a new notification on our phone (hint: turn them off) or a colleague who needs us for "just 5 minutes".

Interruptions are expensive too. In a study from the University of California Irvine, researchers shadowed workers on the job, studying their productivity. Here is what they found:

> "You have to completely shift your thinking, it takes you a while to get into it and it takes you a while to get back and remember where you were...We found about 82 percent of all interrupted work is resumed on the same day. But here's the bad news — it takes an average of 23 minutes and 15 seconds to get back to the task."

We live in a culture obsessed with personal productivity. We devour books on getting things done and dream of four-hour workweeks. We worship at the altar of hustle and boast about being busy. The key to getting things done, we're often told, is time management. If you could just plan your schedule better, you could reach productivity nirvana. But after two decades of studying productivity, I've become convinced that time management is not a solution — it's actually part of the problem.

For most of my career, the most frequent question I've gotten is: "How do I get more done?" Sometimes people ask because they know productivity is one of my areas of expertise.

Being prolific is not about time management. There are a limited number of hours in the day, and focusing on time management just makes us more aware of how many of those hours we waste. A better option is attention management: Prioritize the people and projects that matter, and it won't matter how long anything takes.

Attention management is the art of focusing on getting things done for the right reasons, in the right places and at the right moments.

Time management used to be very similar to attention management. If you designated some time on your calendar to attend to something, it was more likely that thing would get done.

This was back before the digital revolution so thoroughly changed the way information is generated and shared. In other words, before there were so many distractions. Now, the world is constantly available at our fingertips, with the plethora of radio, television, internet, scrolling marquees, skywriting & advertising, not to mention new ways to instantly communicate, and handheld digital devices that are becoming more and more omnipresent.

Allocating time to something no longer means that it will receive your attention, and without attention, your time is somewhat irrelevant. Attention creates action, produces quality and facilitates productivity. Attention also has a dramatic impact on your life. What you give your attention to, is what determines your experiences.

Your Attention Determines Your Life

Think about it…there are entire cultures built around subjects that probably don't even register with you. Don't you know people who are involved in things you know nothing about? Perhaps its monster trucks, vampires, science fiction, or quantum physics. There are people whose lives revolve around subjects that are barely a blip on your radar. Those people give their attention to those topics, and therefore, have experiences around them. And you do the same. So, as William James noted, "your experience is what you agree to attend to." And all of those experiences eventually add up to your life. But most of the time, you don't agree to give your attention; you are just constantly distracted and reacting to all of those things that are vying for your attention. If that's true for you, then maybe you do not have as much control over your life as you might like. This is why attention management is today's most valuable skill.

Consider attention management. Invest in your focus. Support your attention by minimizing distractions. Single task. Learn to meditate. Shut your phone off sometimes, or at least use the Do Not Disturb feature. Put it on silent, NOT vibrate. Close your office door if you have one. Wear headphones if you don't. Stop sabotaging your own focus and attention span, and start supporting your ability to control your attention.

"Always remember, your focus determines your reality."

George Lucasthe tasks that you consider "necessary evils" from your calendar will not only free up your valuable time, it will produce better results, and make you a happier person. Isn't that worth the time it takes to delegate and outsource? Good luck!

Attention Management

While similar to time management, attention management changes the focus of your time to how you are engaging in your work instead of focusing on what you're doing with your time. For instance, did you know that multi-tasking actually hurts your productivity because it takes your brain a significant amount of effort to switch between tasks rapidly?

1. **Reduce distractions so you can focus** - While it's tempting to catch up on emails while watching tv, it can reduce your ability to really zone in and be productive.
2. **Pay attention to your energy throughout the day** - Your motivation to do different tasks changes throughout the day. Listen to your body and work on tasks you like or work on easy tasks during times when you know your energy will be low. Save the tough tasks for when you're feeling rested and motivated. Read the research!
3. **Focus on one thing at a time** - Like we mentioned above, multi-tasking is detrimental to productivity. We know it's so easy to just click into an email that came in while you're working on a deliverable, but we promise 99% of the time, it can wait! Best practice is to work on something for at least 20 minutes before switching to another task.
4. **Be intentional about your time** - None of us want to let anyone down and say, "I'm sorry, but I can't," but if you say yes to everything, you won't be able to give 100% to everything! Give your time a value and be intentional! Read more!
5. **Stay connected to the why** - Feeling unmotivated? Find a reason that intrinsically motivates you. What about this task makes it important? Who does it affect? How will it

makes things better? Intrinsic motivation will get a finished product much faster than extrinsic motivation.

6. **Strengthen your brain's ability to focus** - Of course external factors such as what you work on, distractions, and when you work makes a big difference in your ability to focus, but remember: your brain is a muscle! If you struggle to stay focused, you can improve your ability to focus by practicing! Yoga and meditation are good (and free!) options. If you're super into science and have a little more money to spend, check out neuro-feedback to help "teach" your brain how to focus.

As per Adam Grant, a top professor at The Wharton School of business and an organizational psychologist, "If productivity is your goal you have to rely on willpower to push yourself to get a task done".

And that doesn't get to the heart of the issue. "Often our productivity struggles are caused not by a lack of efficiency, but a lack of motivation," Grant writes.

So instead of focusing on specific tasks, "If you pay attention to why you're excited about the project and who will benefit from it, you'll be naturally pulled into it by intrinsic motivation," he says.

At the right time

Grant says another important component of attention management is taking note of when you get things done: "It's not about time; it's about timing," he says.

Grant points to studies that have found employees are more productive when the weather is bad, for example, because they are "less likely to be distracted by the thought of going outside."

He also references something underscored in Daniel Pink's book "When," which is that your circadian rhythm (aka, whether you're a morning or night person) can help you figure out when is the right time to do productive work, and when is the right time to do creative work.

"It's not time management, because you might spend the same amount of time on the tasks even after you rearrange your schedule," Grant writes in the Times. "It's attention management: You're noticing the order of tasks that works for you and adjusting accordingly."

Grant isn't the only expert to tout the effectiveness of attention management as opposed to time management.

"Better attention management leads to improved productivity, but it's about much more than checking things off a to-do list," productivity expert Maura Thomas wrote in the Harvard Business Review. "The ultimate result is the ability to create a life of choice, around things that are important to you. It's more than just exercising focus. It's about taking back control over your time and your priorities."

Attention Management is the New Time Management

Attention management is getting a lot of traction now, but it's not exactly a new phenomenon. Someone just decided to give it a name.

"We can only be proactive when we're not being reactive"

— **Maura Thomas**

It's important to plan out your day/week/month, schedule your tasks, and take note of your priorities so that you can be as productive as possible. However, you can't actually create more time, so managing your time is more about working with what you've been given and this can sometimes lead to frustration since there are only so many hours in a day!

Attention management is a different story. If you've ever felt like you don't have enough hours in a day to get all of your work completed, attention management offers you a solution by helping you to figure out the most valuable use of the time that you do have.

Rather than focusing on how much time you have, attention management examines what consumes your attention during that time.

When you focus on managing how much attention you give to your projects, you can minimize distractions and ensure that your energy is focused on whatever is most urgent at any given moment. It's all about avoiding distractions when we have multiple things and people vying for our attention. By managing our attention instead of our time, we can decide what we pay attention to and what we can ignore for now. As a result, we can get much more done in the time that we do have.

Motivation is the Root of Attention Management

Everyone knows that the more interested you are in a task the more motivated you'll be to work on it. It's not rocket science. Even time management has recognized this from day one; ever heard of the phrase "eat the frog"? This is a time management ethos that advises you to start your day off with the task you're avoiding the most so that you can stop procrastinating and get moving on the rest of your work, i.e. tasks that you don't find as taxing.

Becoming more efficient at how you manage your tasks is important, let's not undermine that. Creating a workflow, adding Checklists, and setting Reminders, are all super important in order to become and stay productive throughout the day. But whilst efficiency will increase productivity, it's more to do with the fact that being organized in this way makes you more motivated to complete your goals.

So how can you become more motivated? Again, this is where attention management comes in. You have to find the willpower to see a task through to the end and you'll find that by figuring out what excites you about what you're working on. Once you pay attention to why you're doing the task in the first place and how you'll benefit from completing that task — even if it's one small task in a list of many required to reach an end goal — you'll find the intrinsic motivation you need to push forward.

For more on Intrinsic vs Extrinsic Motivation, you can check out this blog post we published on The Key To Success: Positive vs. Negative Motivation which really focuses on the power of finding the passion in what you do.

Work Around your Peak Productivity

Paying attention to how you spend your time will help you to work around your own personal productivity peaks and figure out when you're most productive. Once you've worked that out, you can design your day in a way that best suits your own natural energy levels. The whole early bird/night owl thing is no myth; some people genuinely do their best work at 6 am whilst others don't get that same level of productivity until much later in the day.

By analyzing your productivity peaks, you can optimize your workload to fit in around when you're more likely to excel at different types of work that involve linear or nonlinear thinking. For example, some people may prefer to get their creative work done early in the morning whilst others complete less taxing admin work early in the day so that they can free up their minds to focus on creative work later in the evening.

How to Get the Ball Rolling

It's best to take a week or so to pay attention to how you spend your time, note when you're most motivated to work on specific tasks, figure out what order of tasks works best for you, and adjust your workflow accordingly.

Once you've done this, you can set up a Buckets Project to document all of the info needed to complete each task and set Reminders to ensure you still stay on track. This will help you to balance the best of both worlds when it comes to managing your attention and your time. You'll find more info on how to do this in our blog post: How To Figure Out When You're Most Productive so don't forget to check it out.

"You can't depend on your eyes when your imagination is out of focus."

— **Mark Twain**

		Principle of Time Management & Life Management
		# Let decisions happen automatically and smart decisions will happen by themselves

"On an important decision one rarely has 100% of the information needed for a good decision no matter how much one spends or how long one waits. And, if one waits too long, he has a different problem and has to start all over. This is the terrible dilemma of the hesitant decision maker."

— Robert K. Greenleaf

Automate Decisions

Force your brain to make a lot of decisions and you end up depleting your willpower and suffering from decision fatigue. This hurts your decision-making ability: as the day wears on, you'll start making fewer smart decisions. That's why you are more likely to binge-watch Netflix while eating dinner in the evening.

To avoid mental exhaustion, automate decisions to free yourself from cognitive burden and not rely solely on your self-discipline. Let decisions happen automatically and smart decisions will happen by themselves. Here are examples of smart decisions you can automate:

1. Transfer money to your savings account every time you receive a paycheck
2. Choose all your outfits for your week on Sunday and hang them in the closet in order
3. Subscribe to a weekly fresh delivery of organic vegetables and fruits to your home

4. Standardize the typical daily meals you like the most, saving time in cooking and grocery shopping
5. Prepare your sports bag every night and put in your car. If you prefer running the morning, leave your running shoes near the bed
6. Automate all electronic gadgets to go into sleep mode at a certain hour

You can also automate many other tasks though many of apps available. These apps connect many other apps and let them "talk" to each other, creating automation.

There are not many jobs where you can just sit down and start working without making a prior decision or giving thoughts to how you are going to plan all your work. There are many things to thought upon, like;

➢ Which task is of high-priority
➢ When a task is to be completed
➢ Which resources are available to do the task
➢ Which task need to be done later

All such decisions are to be made before you sit to work, so a task doesn't affect another task. This is a one kind of a time management strategy which if done wrong can bring a zero outcome for the day. Make clear decisions related to your tasks to greatly improve the way you have to work.

Several types of decisions help reduce the stress of urgency, deadlines and high demands on your time. Poor allocation of your time is the result of poor decisions and can lead to mistakes as you progress toward your goals. Errors take time to correct and can lead to an ongoing cycle of more stress, greater urgency and ultimately more mistakes. Decision-making is crucial to time management.

Deciding on Now

We all share the same amount of linear time dictated by clocks and calendars. Nobody has more hours in a day or days in the year than anyone else. However, time is also a subjective experience of what is happening to you right now. Deciding to focus primarily on your subjective experience of time in the present moment, and only secondarily on your clock and calendar deadlines, gives you flexibility to get more done in a scheduled time frame. For example, a two-hour meeting will be two hours long no matter what happens during it. However, the value of the meeting isn't controlled by how long it lasts but by how focused, productive and results-oriented the participants are.

Aligning Priorities

Choosing what's most important gives you a structure by which you can organize your day. Your daily tasks may change, but your top goals and values are more important and lasting. Your priorities, then, are the tasks that most align with your goals and values. The less control you have over your priorities, the more likely it is that you'll spend too much time on distractions rather than productive activities. Taking time to decide on, and regularly review, your professional and organizational goals and values will help you prioritize your daily to-do list, while helping you realize and eliminate less important tasks and distractions that may be intruding on your time.

Lightening the Load

Delegating or automating some of the tasks you are responsible for is crucial to time management. Whether to outsource tasks, automate a process within your department, use technology to streamline some of your routine work, enlist help on tasks or delegate them to employees are decisions that apply to how you manage your personal workload. Pacing yourself and staying on top of your work can keep you in control of your schedule. You can stay focused more on the appointments and activities most aligned with your goals.

Lifestyle Decisions

Your overall lifestyle decisions contribute to your level of effective time management on and off the job. Eating right, getting enough rest, staying hydrated and exercising can help you sharpen your mind, have more energy and improve your problem-solving abilities. Scheduling quality family time, personal growth activities such as reading or meditation, hobbies, fun with friends, or the occasional work vacation can help ensure you have balance in your life. This can lead to better decisions on the job and less stress about time.

Automation can be a huge time saver. It can automate repetitive or mundane tasks, increasing efficiency. However, automation should never replace the conversation. You never want to push so much out through automation that you take the "social" out of social media.

What you can do with automation is schedule upcoming content to maintain a consistent posting schedule. There are many tools that can help you view your scheduled messages for the day, week, or month, to make sure you fill the gaps between posts. Whatever the tool you decide on, let it assist you in building relationships and creating meaningful conversation. It should help, not hurt your daily efforts.

Automation tools can expand your presence while allowing you to stay engaged and involved in your growing community.

"As technology advances, it reverses the characteristics of every situation again and again. The age of automation is going to be the age of 'do it yourself.'"

— **Marshall McLuhan**

		Principle of Time Management & Life Management
 **19**		# Always see the Bigger Picture
Long-Term Planning yield huge rewards

"It is important to ask yourself why you're doing what you're doing and what purpose it serves in the big picture."

However tight things are, you still need to have the big picture at the forefront of your mind.

Thinking Ahead & Bigger Picture

Not everyone works solely on a day-to-day basis. Many people have to operate in a way that involves keeping in mind a span of time that may be weeks, months, or even years in extent. Here, a particular approach can enhance the practicality of a diary.

This might appropriately be called the opposite of the "if only . . ." school of ineffective time management. Too often managers find themselves in a crisis that would be all too easily resolved if they could wind the clocks back. We surely all know the feeling. "If only we had done so and so earlier," we say as we contemplate a messy and time-consuming process of unscrambling. In all honesty, though the unexpected can happen sometimes, crisis management is all too common . . . and often all too unnecessary. Coping well with crises that are, for whatever reason, upon us saves time; certainly if the alternative is panic.

If you can acquire the habit of thinking ahead and take a systematic view of things, then you are that much more likely to see when a start really needs to be made on something. If things are left late or ill thought out (and the two can often go together), then time is used up in a hasty attempt to sort things out at short notice. This tends to make any task more difficult and is compounded by whatever day-to-day responsibilities are current at the time.

- Some people find that to "see" the pattern of future work and tasks in their mind's eye can be difficult. One invaluable aid to this is the planning or wall chart.
- Whatever you do to document things, however, the key is to get into the habit of thinking ahead—at the same time and without disrupting the current day's workload. Anticipating problems and spotting opportunities can make a real difference to the way you work in the short term.

The mental process of seeing a span of time, rather than thumbing through pages, is really helpful in managing any kind of project. For example, the production of this book spanned many months, involving time allocated to writing, typesetting and printing with tasks such as reading proofs scheduled in along the way. Care here can prevent missed deadlines and that can save more than time.

Be careful of taking time in duplication. For instance, some people enter everything in three places: a diary, a planning chart, and a separate wall planner. Additional recording may be necessary too, such as a separate chart to plan and monitor people's holidays. If you want to use a planning chart as your sole diary device, why not do so? The key is to keep a handle on the whole of your schedule no matter what length of time this encompasses. All such decisions are to be made before you sit to work, so a task doesn't affect another task. This is a one kind of a time management strategy which if done wrong can bring a zero outcome for the day. Make clear decisions related to your tasks to greatly improve the way you have to work.

"If you just focus on the smallest details, you will never get the big picture right."

— **Leory Hood**

Principle of Time Management & Life Management

20 Don't let Evil Side of Internet ruin you

Internet or call it Social Media is something that has become a real hazard in recent years and must waste uncounted hours in offices around the world.

The internet: or, more specifically, non-work-related surfing or Social Networking Sites (SNS).

Social media have effects on student's time management?

According to the survey, when student or even common man come to connect and analyze the questions about the dedication of time spent on important chores, studying, and social media platforms you realize that, on the choice that says "not on a daily basis" only 4% spend their day without using any of the Social Networking Sites (SNS) while 17% do not study on daily basis and 19% do not perform other important chores in a student's life.

Results are almost equal on the "less than an hour" choice with 11% for using social media 11% for studying and 19% for other important chores. At one to two hours the results favor the studying and other important chores more with 44% for both and only 37% for social media.

What is more disturbing that when the hours increased, the usage of social media increased and the time spent on studying and other important chores decreased drastically after reaching their peak. On three to four hours, 30% spend time on SNS while 20% spend studying and only 9% perform important chores. 9% said that they perform important chores for more than four hours and 7% said they spend more than four hours studying while 19% use social media platforms for more than hours.

Are the students aware of the effects the SNS have on their time management?

After constructing a study on if the students are aware by the effects the social networking sites have on their time management I realized that they are somehow mostly aware. That is what made me wonder more and more, because if the students are unaware then maybe the parents must be blamed for the effects I found in my research paper, but after finding out that students know how much these sites have effects and they do not try to resist it then the students have to be blamed for that.

There are billions of people all around the world that use social media. Some of them visit such platforms as Facebook or Instagram for several minutes. The others may "hang" there for a couple of hours. Finally, there are some individuals who spend most of the day over there. It is especially true when we talk about students. They seem to spend every free minute in social media and it's a matter of great concern of many educators and parents.

One of the main negative consequences is time management.

"One day you will look back and recall all the time you spent on social media and wonder why you didn't invest that time someplace else."

— **Germany Kent**

Social Media Steals the Time on Learning

Different studies were carried out to define how social media affect students time management. Most of them agree that it steals a lot of precious time. Students get absorbed by various platforms and lose interest in their studies. Regardless of the purpose, they hang there, the priorities of students strongly change.

Why do students spend and, let's be honest, waste their time on social media? They access interactive content that matches their preferences. These are videos, audios, a discussion of various teenage topics, and of course, pure chatting with one another. It is said that friendship is a lengthy period that also absorbs time.

Nevertheless, digital communication doesn't bring too many dividends for youngsters.

It isn't real and people act differently when they meet in reality. Texting is much faster and simultaneously, it takes more time. Young people don't even realize how many hours they waste on socializing via the Internet. They may think "I'll quickly send a few responses and that will do". Unfortunately, they begin to look for other interlocutors just to continue their chatting. It's important to communicate with your peers. Nevertheless, if students overdo, they have no time for their homework tasks.

There are the following problems related to social media and time management:

- Loss of interest in studies and other spheres of life.
- Avoidance of responsibilities.
- Laziness.
- Social isolation.
- Distraction from studies.
- An inability to gain a proper concentration.
- Worsening of learning results.
- A decrease in learning abilities.

Every academic task has a clear deadline. If a student violates them, he or she loses a lot of grades. Besides, there are different subjects and a limited number of hours given to master the material. If they are inattentive during their classes or even miss them, they will never learn what is required.

Students steadily lose their grip. Their skills remain at the same level and due to a lack of practice those skills worsen. Students aren't interested in any sort of academic competition and lose any interest. Even when they try to study, they get distracted by a continuous desire to review a few videos or send a couple of messages. They lose the possibility to focus on any task for a long period of time. Students become obsessed with social media and this is a real mental deviation.

"The more screen-time you consume on your device, the more revenue can the big tech make. So, your health, your wellbeing, your sanity and serenity are nowhere closer to their priorities. That's why, your health is in your hands, your serenity is in your hands, your sanity is in your hands."

Besides, social media "obsession" leads to many other negative consequences. Therefore, students and their parents ought to be cautious. They are supposed to act reasonably and limit time spent on social media. Otherwise, they risk falling behind their academic programs.

The idea is simple: don't engage in non-work-related surfing. Actually, that needs some discipline and resolve. After all, the internet is a source of information. An hour ago, before writing this, I logged on to Google to get directions to an office at which I have just set a meeting, a company website to check out the kind of business they were in, and another to book an air ticket. All represented a good, time-efficient way of doing these little jobs, but . . . let me be honest, despite the fact that I'm writing about time management, I was tempted. While my Word file was tucked away at the bottom of the screen, all I had to do was click on Favorites and just slip in one more task (there's a book I want to order from Amazon, for instance).

The worst time-waster in this area is probably social websites such as Facebook. Time very quickly disappears as you dip "just once more" into a chat site. And if you doubt the danger and want another thought that might reinforce the truth, it is reckoned that a high percentage of all the hits on pornographic sites are made between 9 a.m. and 5 p.m. when presumably most computer users are at work!

- ➤ Be aware of the likely distraction and resolve to avoid temptation.
- ➤ Don't put sites that you may like and use in private into the Favorites file in your work computer.
- ➤ Follow your organization's guidelines—rules—about this sort of thing; they are there for a reason.

Internet interferes with time management

What happen to us when we use the Internet and how they impact upon your ability to manage time.

1. **Altered sense of time.** Using the Internet appears to distort our sense of time. In studies where people have been asked to perform an online task and report how long it took them once they had finished, they regularly underestimate the time taken. What people believe took them "about five minutes" tends to last about 25 minutes.
2. **Repetitive working.** People tend to do the same thing more than once when using online technologies. They read an email. Then go back to it some hours later to read it again and deal with it. Or people visit a web page, save it as a bookmark and then go back on another date to read it again. The Internet encourages "double work".
3. **Poor searching.** Around one in three people who search for something never click on any of the results provided. They realize that these search results are not what they wanted and so revisit their search engine again to search for different words. Even when a search result is clicked on, around 80% of people revisit the search engine to perform another search as they were not satisfied with the results. Repetitive searching due to poor search behaviour is estimated to be taking most people an hour each day.
4. **Lack of concentration.** The Internet is one of the main providers of "sensory overload". This can happen when our senses just find it difficult to cope with any more input. Sensory overload can lead to a range of symptoms including irritability, restlessness and poor sleep. However, one of the main effects is a difficulty to concentrate. The more you use the Internet the less capable you become at concentrating on your work, plus it hampers your ability to remember things.
5. **Sleep deprivation.** Internet users are frequently sleep-deprived. Often they are checking for messages late at night, which can make the brain's timing mechanisms prevent the start of sleep. When sleep does come, it is generally poor quality and the next day the Internet user is too tired to pay proper attention to things or to make good decisions.

With the world at your fingertips, it seems that there is not enough time to explore the Internet, but you need Internet time management to get things done daily. You may not realize it, but time spent using the Internet is usually just wasted time, making you unproductive and resulting in delayed output or nothing done at all. Strategy to make some changes to stop wasting time online.

1. Define Your Need

Ask yourself why you are using the Internet. If you are using it for work, like doing research, making reports, performing write ups or writing articles, then Internet use is essential. But, if you are in front of the computer just keeping yourself updated with the latest news on social networking or online gaming, then you are just wasting your time and should rethink your daily activities.

2. Focus on Your Need

Before sitting in front of your computer or laptop, make a schedule of your Internet time or better yet your daily activity schedule. With this schedule, you know how much time you need to use the Internet. Focusing on the things you need to do before doing them gives you the motivation to finish your tasks on time. This way you reduce the time wasted on Internet usage that is not necessary.

3. Limit Guilt Free Internet Use

Now you have decided to revamp your internet usage to needs only, but it doesn't mean that you can't use the Internet for your own entertainment. Spare yourself some time out of the day to do it. Thirty minutes will do just for that. Buy a stopwatch or alarm clock if you need to. Divide your time from the different sites you like to browse. You don't even have to read the latest news; chances are, if its top news it will always be talked about everywhere and for sure you can catch that news from somebody.

4. Schedule Other Activities Offline

If you are getting ahead and not wasting time in front of the computer, it does not mean that you have an excuse to sit in front of the television. Stop wasting your time looking at other people's lives unfolding, but do start to make a name for yourself. If you have the resources, get yourself into a class that you like, cooking or the arts. If not, start a new hobby like running for causes or the like. People nowadays are becoming health buffs; maybe it will work for you too. Get socially involved as well.

Internet is an essential tool for most people today but somehow there are still those who do not realize that they are wasting time using it. Managing Internet time usage is a great help to your lifestyle not just by helping you become more effective in your daily life but it can also improve your productivity as a whole. With Internet time management, you can make yourself be more focused on the important aspects of life.

Why time management techniques won't work

Time management techniques include the need to set priorities and to timetable activities. However, when the impact of the Internet is taken into consideration this is not always easy. For a start, the effects of sleep deprivation and lack of concentration caused by sensory overload mean that it can be difficult to set priorities. As a result, people are prioritizing things without much in-depth thought, which in turn means that some things may be inaccurately prioritized, inevitably messing up the time management plan.

Timetables also face pressure when people underestimate the amount of time taken to complete online tasks. It's no good having a neatly laid out diary or online calendar if the Internet tasks you undertake then interfere with your timetable. Indeed, that appears to be leading to another phenomenon of the Internet – constantly re-timetabling.

That suggests that more people are beginning to realize that their time management efforts are not working, or that they need to find out how to manage time better because their day never really works out as planned.

The way we use the Internet is at the heart of this issue.

Coping when time management techniques do not work is not about finding some kind of time management app (another popular search) or taking yet another time management training course or watching another YouTube video on the topic. Instead, coping starts with understanding our personal motivations for the way we use the Internet.

Another issue with attitudes to the way we use the Internet is assuming that search engines will find whatever we want, however, we search for it. That simply is not true. Search engines need you to be quite detailed with your search term. The algorithms are good but they are not psychic. Understanding that search engines are comparatively weak means you are more likely to use advanced search techniques which will ultimately save your time. If you continue in the false belief that search engines can find exactly what you want, then you will spend more time searching than you appreciate, impacting upon your time management.

Time management techniques require you to be relatively organized in the first place. The way we use the Internet and the impact of the technology on our behavior means that our ability to manage time is hampered, no matter which techniques you use. Only by getting to grips with the way we use the Internet will we be able to use time management techniques effectively in our digital world.

Turn off all notifications on your phone, except the most important ones. And check your social media only once or twice a day, not every minute. If you can do this, then perhaps there is a possibility, that society will not completely lose its sanity and health after all.

Sole Purpose of Life is to be Happy.

Happiness Mantra 5 – Don't React immediately when provoked

Whenever you feel disturbed or restless due to some sudden problems or some irrelevant remarks or comments by somebody, avoid reacting immediately or coming under sudden provocations. Allow sometime to pass and refrain from doing or saying anything as long as disturbance persists in your mind. It is best if you temporarily avoid the person or situation whom you consider the cause of your disturbance. Preferably go away from that place and sit silently in solitude for sometime. Slow down and cool down yourself and then examine coolly all pros and cons. You are more likely to understand better about the real problem in this state of mind. Under provocation, the reasoning power of the mind gets destroyed.

Give clarifications to people of your innocence only when asked for. Don't force your innocence on people. You voice in reply should always be polite, respectful and controlled. You should never behave in an uncontrolled fashion and not resort to shouting while replying, howsoever wrong blame or criticism has been done to you.

Principle of Time Management & Life Management

 Group Similar Tasks Together for Awesome Time Management

For a case - If you are running out to grab something at the office supply store, make sure that you review anything else that might need to be done along the same driving path.

As I need to grab some more toner for my laser printer. Rather than running out and only getting the ink, I looked at my other to-dos and the route I would be taking to get to the store.

As a result, I stopped at our insurance agent to sign some papers, made a deposit at the bank, filled up my tank with gas and grabbed the ink. In this example the items were alike because they were all on the same driving path that I needed to take to get to the office supply store.

Task-Batching as a useful 'structural element' to implement to enhance time management.

If you look away from your computer screen for even a second, your eyes are introduced to a world of distractions. Your phone, chatting coworkers and many other, often self-imposed mental interruptions are the plague of productivity. It's amazing what people can get done nowadays, considering a lot of things near and far are calling for our attention. Imagine the work you could accomplish if you had a strategy for blocking off time for specific tasks.

Enter time batching.

What's the first thing you do in the morning? Open your emails, right? You take each email one by one, opening each, completing the task that it invites, and responding to it. You cycle through this process for the next hour and a half maybe, intermittently picking up the phone, hanging up, and asking yourself that famous question that signals a distraction: 'ah, where was I?'.

Each of these interruptions and switches of task causes a lapse of focus. It has been reported that interruptions can take as much as twenty-five minutes to recover from! Let's look at an example within your personal life and then relate it back to business.

> *Say you plan your Saturday to be a fun day full of chores around the house. You need to organize your closet, fold laundry, and do the dishes. You wouldn't clean three plates, go fold a shirt, and then pick which drawer you want your socks to be held in, would you? No. Because it wouldn't make any sense or be very time efficient. If you were to practice time batching, you would pair cleaning your closet with folding your laundry (because both of these tasks include clothes) and then do the dishes after.*
>
> *Now your day at the office - you need to put together a presentation, send 10 emails, and write a report. You wouldn't make two presentation slides, send four emails, and then write the introduction to your report, right? It wouldn't be the worst thing in the world, but continuously switching activities and refocusing your attention is a gigantic time suck.*

To start, task batching simply means – grouping similar tasks together in order to get them done more efficiently. I like to use these two criteria:

> ➢ **Mental mode** – In other words, the state of mind that you're in. When you group tasks of a similar mental mode together, you can enter a state of flow and get through them faster. For example: Don't task batch writing a blog newsletter with editing a YouTube video (even though they're both blog-related). Instead, task batch writing a blog post with writing an article for the school newspaper. The common thread? Writing.

> **Location/resources** – Consider where you need to be and what you need to do to complete the task. For example, completing your math worksheet and your biology homework might require the same mental mode for you. Check. However, if you need a library computer for the biology assignment and you can only focus on your math homework when you're alone, that task batch simply won't work.

Batching tasks together

This time management technique is slightly different – and its power comes from its disarming simplicity. Really, the idea boils down to one notion: that you can focus better – and get things done quicker – by doing similar tasks at the same time.

I am a fan of **FOCUS – Follow One Course Until Successful.**

So rather than flicking from email to phone call to meeting to spreadsheet, keep all the different types of task together. This prevents you from expending your effort switching gear, in moving from one type of task to the next – those movements which impede your focus and get you stuck in those twenty-five unproductive minutes of lost focus and procrastination.

Change the way you think about your work

The reality of work is that you probably don't just have the one project on the go. You won't have a simple straight line of a step by step process you need to follow. Rather, as David Allen observed in his blog on Getting Things Done, we all have roughly thirty projects that we are juggling at any one time. And all of these different projects involve very similar tasks: planning; coordination with your colleagues, staff, and partners; writing blogs or reports maybe. And all these different types of task require a particular way of thinking, a particular action different from each other.

Why does time batching work?

People see success with time batching because it eliminates the presence of multi-tasking. Multi-tasking, or dealing with more than

one task at the same time, is a productivity killer. Don't take it from me, take it from science, and few different studies on multitasking and business:
- Multitasking can lead to as much as a 40% drop in productivity.
- People who are interrupted and have to switch their attention back and forth take 50% longer to complete a task.
- Multitaskers make up to 50% more errors when completing a task.

Building (metaphorical) structures and boundaries with your time make it easier to dive into a task or group of tasks without breaking your workflow.

Time Batching – Benefit to whom?

The beauty of time batching is that it can be used by just about anybody - no matter your job, industry, or role in life. Anyone that is looking to have a productive day and feel satisfied at the end of the day should incorporate time batching into their time management techniques. Time batching can be used to separate any task, but they are often split into two categories: shallow and deep.
- A shallow task is an activity that is quick, easy, and doesn't require much energy.
- A deep task is a lengthy project that is going to require a lot more time and energy.

When time batching, you can find a like group of shallow tasks and knock them all out at once during a certain period of time. On the other hand, you can also set aside a specific amount of time to make some progress on a deep task. Either way, you will achieve a state of flow where you are in the zone and making the most of your time.

Here are some signs you should be using time batching:
- You find it hard to concentrate on a single task
- You get distracted easily
- Your work environment is full of disturbances
- You regularly repeat certain tasks

> Your regular tasks are all related and can be categorized together

How to task-batch

The technique of task-batching suggests that you divide your day by the different types of task that you need to complete – and strive to complete them in the time you've allotted.

1. Determine your tasks

Before batching, you need to first see what kind of tasks you are working with. This step essentially includes writing a to-do list where you get a clear picture of what your day/week/month is going to look like. If you are going to be using time batching for both personal and professional tasks, make sure to keep them separate.

2. Batch your tasks

With your list in front of you, find related tasks would make sense to do one right after the other. Remember there is no limit to the amount of tasks that can fit into a certain batch, but there should be a realistic time frame. Even though the point of time batching is to help your attention span, we can only stay fully focused for so long before we need a break to eat, use the bathroom, or get some fresh air.

Say you have 30 similar tasks to do in your marketing automation tool. You estimate that it will take 3 hours. That's a long time to be fully focused. In cases like this, there is nothing wrong with splitting those tasks even further into two batches of 15 projects that will take an hour and a half each.

3. Evaluate your process

After you have completed your time batching tasks, assess how well you did. This is something that is going to take some time and practice, and being a perfect time batcher after the first go around is not likely. After doing it a couple of times, you will learn more about yourself as a doer. How long can you actually stay focused? (This is different for everyone and there is no shame in your answer). Is there a sweet spot for the amount of tasks you can do within that time frame? Is there an order you like to follow? Do you prefer to do big or small tasks first?

Tips for Time Batching

Focusing on only batching your time is a good place to start, but there are some tips that will make the experience even more productive.

1. Batch realistically

The point of time batching is to group similar tasks together for a more productive day. However, sometimes it makes more sense to complete tasks together that aren't so similar. For example, say you need to go to the gym and do some grocery shopping. If the grocery store is on the way home from the gym, it makes perfect sense to do those activities back to back, even though they aren't necessarily similar.

2. Set clear goals

Setting due dates and holding yourself accountable to completing them is necessary to time batch successfully. Having an end date/time will motivate you that much more when trying to be productive. If you set loose time parameters, you will keep pushing it back and cut yourself too much slack. When setting these goals, make sure you write them down. A Harvard Business study found that people that write their goals down are three times as likely to complete them.

3. Use the right tools

In the age of technology, there are countless tools that can help you stay organized when time batching. Project management software is the perfect tool for handling a lot of tasks at once. It manages both short and long term projects, enables collaboration on tasks, and analyzes productivity. If online tools aren't your favorite, you can always get a physical calendar and write everything down. Or hey, why not do both?

4. Eliminate distractions where you can

Time batching is meant to eliminate distractions that come about when we go are constantly transitioning from one task to another. However, there are plenty of other distractions that we face during our day to day. Phones, TVs, friends, loud spaces- there is an abundance of distractions while working, and it is your job to get rid of them. Mute that cell phone, turn off the TV or radio, and find a quiet place to work. This will only help you.

5. Share your plans

If you work with a team or around a lot of other people, let them know that you are time batching for however long and would prefer to not be disturbed. Make it clear that the purpose of this time management technique is to eliminate distractions and stay focused. This way, they will think twice before reaching out to you during your designated time batching period.

Task-batching for big projects

If there is a big task that you need to complete, the principle of task-batching suggests that you should do a large part – if not all – of it at once. Think through the project, split it into chunks that can be completed in two-hour slots and schedule these in your diary, blocking the time and outlining the part of the task to be completed in each slot.

Remember, turn off your phone, your email, your social media feeds. With dedicated time comes focus.

Other applications?

Honestly, you can time-batch with almost every task you can think of. You could buy all your groceries once a week to prevent the endless back and forth from the shops. You could, as people are doing more and more, make lots of meals at once and freeze them – to free up the rest of your evenings.

So, what does this have to do with 'structure' in your business?

A major structural element in your business is how you communicate with each other and interact during your day. As the business owner, you dictate the rules and policies around this: the expected response times, habits, practices, methods of communication, and if your staff can have 'protected time' where they are not interrupted, etc.

This is all down to you both implementing and enforcing these initiatives. Have you reviewed these practices? Have you consulted with your staff about the best ways they work? How quickly is someone expected to respond to an email or message? How do you use email in your organisation?

These are all questions to ask, to begin the conversation around more effective working practices and greater efficiency in your business. It won't be easy in the beginning, but do persevere. As with all things, the long-term advantages will be worth the initial pain!

 "If you don't like what you are reaping, then you need to check what you are sowing."

The main idea behind this time management technique is to collect up a group of similar activities and do them all in one swoop. You can work efficiently on multiple tasks without losing your flow if the activities require similar mindsets. Batching forces your brain to be focused on one type of task at a time. Batch similar tasks and complete them at one time. Batching reduces the start-up and slow-down time, daily clutter, and improves focus.

"Batching Similar Task" is a highly useful tool that can help you be more productive in your work or personal life. Productivity experts routinely advocate planning all your errands together so that you aren't wasting gas or time making multiple trips.

Think about the work you do on a weekly or month basis. Obviously some things are not prone to batching, such as a weekly progress report or sales update. But when you consider the repetitive tasks that most workplaces include, there are probably some tasks that could easily be batched. There are several methods for "batching".

Daily

As you look at your to-do list for the day, consider if there are some tasks that would make sense to batch. For example, many workers benefit from specifying certain times to check and return email or choosing to return phone calls all together. Are you constantly up and down scanning or copying things? Make a folder and put things in it throughout the day, if you don't need something right away, so that you don't forget what you wanted to copy, but you are taking care of your admin tasks at once.

By Output

You also can batch things according to weekly or monthly outputs. For example, I write blog posts like this one every week. What if I set aside one morning and did all four for the month at once? Then the next morning I could tackle posts or articles for another writing client.

By Process

Using the example above, instead of going to start to finish on one post, I could look at my writing deadlines for the week and schedule by tasks, so that it looked like this:

There are many productivity benefits to batching:

- **Less "ramp up" time.** Whether you're logging into special software, pulling up template reports or even just calling up your phone directory to find a number, taking care of similar tasks at once eliminates the start/stop effort.
- **Increased focus.** When I am writing, I am concentrating completely on the writing process and not worrying about email or the other tasks that can catch my attention. When I batch by process, as described above, I am focused in "research" mode or "writer" mode. When I am looking for research it's just as easy to pull up articles on multiple topics as to do one, shut down the browser and then do another.
- **A sense of satisfaction.** When you have like tasks that you do repeatedly, it's easy to feel as though you have never actually finished anything because there's always another one waiting. By batching all your invoicing together it's a huge task you can cross off your to-do list! Your own personal sense of accomplishment can help you decide if batching by output or process is preferable. Some people would prefer a whole task crossed off their list (one whole

article done) while others, like me, find it useful to have all the research done and notes assembled to make the most of writing time.
- ➢ **Reduces mental clutter.** Avoiding multitasking helps your brain stay calm and focused, even on your busiest days.
- ➢ **Relieves stress.** Having a big task ahead can be daunting. Using time batching to tackle it in an orderly and practical way will help reduce that stress.

"Time is money." *"I don't happen to agree. While money is important — I think time is way more important and precious than money. Because time is what our lives are made of. And too many people are trading it for money.all."*

— **Robert Kiyosaki**

		**Principle of Time Management & Life Management**
		# It is what you don't do, that matters

 World is changing very fast, so like we have to change our ancient principles which we are following up. In today's world, it is more important to know what you don't need to do, and be firm on not doing that.

This is the proven advice shared by most of successful CEOs.

"We need to do a better job of putting ourselves higher on our own 'to do' list." - Michelle Obama

To-Do lists are so popular they need no introduction. You're surrounded by them: at the grocery store, around the house, even in outer space! But where is your Not-To-Do List.

In Mathematics, there is a problem-solving technique called "inversion".

You start with results and work backward to calculate the causes. Inversion is a powerful tool because it forces you to uncover hidden beliefs about the problem you are trying to solve. You need to think how to minimize the negatives instead of maximizing the positives.

Let's say you want to improve productivity. Thinking forward, you would list all the things you could do to be more productive. But if you look at the problem by inversion, you'd think about all the things you could do that would diminish productivity.

Enter the To-Don't List.

Create your own by writing down all the habits you want to quit and the activities you wish to eliminate from your life. Think about your possible workday — long meetings with people you don't like and boring repetitive tasks — and work from there.

Create a To-Don't list with all the habits you want to remove from your life. Use it as a guideline of what you don't allow in your life.

Here are a couple of examples:
- ➢ Do not email first thing in the morning or last thing at night
- ➢ No morning meetings
- ➢ Don't say yes unless you're 100% certain you can deliver
- ➢ Don't drink coffee in the afternoon
- ➢ Do not agree to meetings or calls with no clear agenda or end time

The reason why inversion works is simple: **what you don't do determines what you can do.**

> *"People think focus means saying yes to the thing you've got to focus on. But that's not what it means at all. It means saying no to the hundred other good ideas that there are. Innovation is saying no to 1,000 things."*
>
> — **Steve Jobs**

"If you want balance in your life, you want a Not-to-Do list."

— **Michael Hyatt**

Remember, the To-Do list tendency is to grow and grow.

Do you have a to-do list? Of course--most of us do. But, what about a not-to-do list? It turns out that's at least as important, according to productivity experts. What exactly is a not-to-do list?

It's not a list of bad habits you're determined to break or negative behavior you want to be sure to avoid. It's a list of tasks that you might think you should do, or might want to do, or might be asked to do by someone else. But because these tasks don't move you toward any of your larger objectives, don't feed your soul, and aren't necessary for you to do, you are much better off not doing them. They should either be left undone or you should delegate them to someone else.

The most successful people I know say that great careers arise out of what you say no to. It makes sense because time and energy is a limited resource for each of us and how we choose to spend that precious resource matters a lot. Management consultant and executive coach writes in the Harvard Business Review:

> *"Once you accept that you have more to do than time to do it all, that is actually a liberating concept. This realization forces you to acknowledge there are lower priority items that you will likely never complete. Delete those non-essentials, put them on your not-to-do list, and commit to letting them go. This will prevent you from wasting precious time continually re-evaluating whether you might get to them that could be better invested in actually completing your work."*

A not-to-do list will bring you clarity and peace because there will be less shame and anxiety over things you think you should do, or worse, have told someone else you will do, but are having trouble getting to. It will also bring greater transparency and improve your relationships with your colleagues and customers because you will no longer be making promises you can't keep.

> *"The only way for a super-productive person to continue to grow professionally without going crazy is to periodically decide what you are not going to do."*
>
> — **Michael Hyatt**

 	Principle of Time Management & Life Management
	# Multitasking is a Myth

Just imagine. You put social meeting in your calendar, taking time away from your to-do list.

When you get there, you check your cell phone just before heading in and something HORRENDOUS has happened, you lost a client or a sale, or your bank sent you a notice that your account was hacked, whatever. **Now you have to go in there and "be social". Is it going to happen? Never. Multitasking is a myth.**

Multitasking is a corporate myth that has evolved over time. *Multi-tasking is way of function of a machine, not for human.* According to the Mirriam Webster Dictionary, multitasking is:

The concurrent performance of several jobs by a computer (notice the computer part) the performance of multiple tasks at one time.

Recent psychological studies have shown that multi-tasking does not actually save time. In fact, the opposite is often true. You lose time when switching from one task to another, resulting in a loss of productivity.

The brain is designed to focus on one thing at a time. Switching between tasks can have damaging costs to our work and productivity. Routine multi-tasking may lead to difficulty in concentrating and maintaining focus when needed.

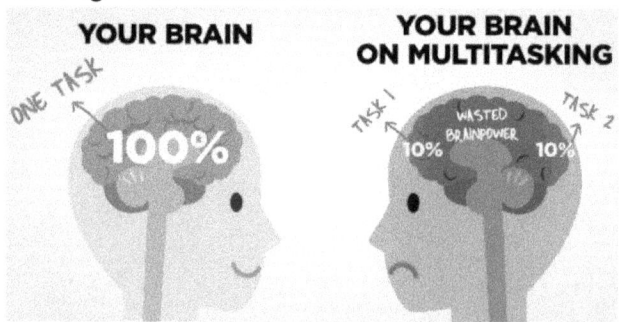

Time Management is Life Management

Messing two things up at the same time, isn't multitasking.

When I was younger, I, like many young entrepreneurs, prided myself on being a master at multitasking. I thought I needed to be a strong multitasker to optimize efficiency and productivity at every moment. And I thought that everyone who was successful got to where they were by being great multitaskers. But, the truth is, there's really no such thing as multitasking.

Most of us think of multitasking as a necessary part of life. How else could we possibly meet the demands of our over-scheduled, hectic lives? But, the truth is, you can only truly multitask (accomplish more than one task simultaneously) if:

> One or more of the tasks is "second nature". In other words, it is so well-learned that no real thought is necessary to complete the task, like chewing gum or walking.

> The tasks being performed involve different brain processes. For instance, if you're reading a book, you can listen to classical (instrumental) music at the same time, but if you listen to music with lyrics, you won't retain as much of the information you're reading. This is because both reading and listening to songs with words activate the language center of the brain. And the brain literally cannot process more than one task in any given category at a time.

Develop the habit of single-tasking by forcing your brain to concentrate on one task and one task only. Put your phone away, close all the browser windows and apps that you don't need. Immerse yourself in this task. Only move to the next one when you're done.

Force your brain to single task in order to do Deep Work and avoid task switching costs.

As per James Clear, Quality of work done is inversely proportional to the amount of multi-tasking.

Time Management is Life Management

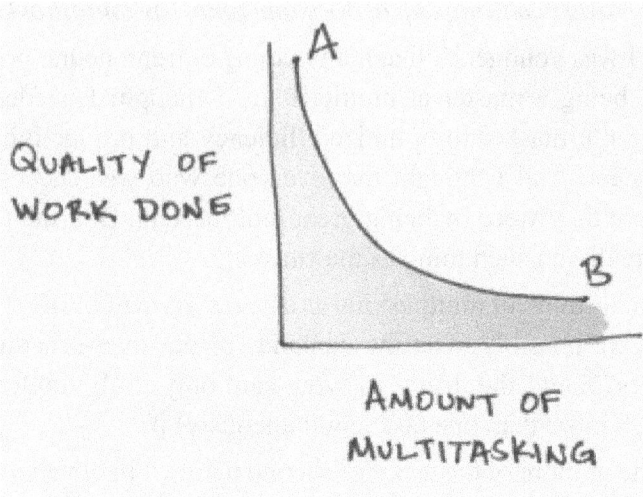

A = Looks simple, but actually gets results.
B = Looks busy, but actually wastes time.

 *"If you chase two rabbits at the same time both are going to get away."*

— **A Proverb**

Time management and multitasking are opposites of each other.

The idea that you, as a human, can concentrate and be effective doing multiple tasks at once is the height of hubris and impossible! Multitasking is the erroneous thought that you can accomplish two things at once.

In the real world, you can only do one thing at a time effectively. Think about it, while brain surgeons performing surgery they do not monitor their cell phones to see if they got an email or check their texts to see if someone sent them a message. They do one thing, surgery.

Doing one thing at a time is hard. It requires that you "live in the now" and pay attention to what you are doing or who is around you. It requires that you get over thinking that it is selfish to do what you want, when you want (or need) to do it. It requires closing doors, turning off phones and concentrating or turning off phones and paying attention to the people who are near you.

One of the things that is so striking to me is how brilliant people are perceived and how they became successful. I have heard about Steve Jobs, Bill Gates and Richard Branson that one of the amazing things about them is that they were present when they talked to people. When someone they met says, "they acted like I was the only person in the room", what they are really saying is that they paid attention to them. Mostly it comes with the note that the time was under a minute, but just that attention for a minute made a huge difference.

Multitasking and Work

Okay, this is a huge one. Common lore says you can accomplish more if you are doing multiple work projects at the same time, either small todos all at once, or big projects over the same timeline. You switch back and forth, miraculously accomplishing twice as much as you would if you did one thing, finished it and then moved onto the next. Seriously, this DOES NOT HAPPEN. What happens is you then have more things, partly done and nothing is FINISHED.

Try this for a week. Make a list of the top three things that are the highest and best use of your time for your business today (mine today are: write a blog post, check, scan back two contracts, not yet, and do client work). These are a mix of moving my business forward (getting new eyeballs on my website with a blog post), working on my business (getting contracts finalized) and doing my "job" in my business (doing client work). Too often we take our eyes off the big picture and get mired in how much work we have to do. My to-do list is crazy like yours, but there is no sense whining about it, just do those three things and then move on to the next most important three things like the little engine that could and you will move forward I promise!

We all do Multi-tasking, though it is illusion only: Texting while walking, sending emails during meetings, chatting on the phone while cooking dinner. In today's society, doing just one thing at a time seems downright luxurious, even wasteful.

But chances are, you're not doing yourself (or your boss, or your friends and family) any favors by multitasking your way through the day. Research shows that it's not nearly as efficient as we like to believe, and can even be harmful to our health.

Rethink the way you work, socialize, and live your life – Stop Multi-tasking

1. You're not really multitasking

What you call multitasking is really task-switching, says Guy Winch, PhD, author of Emotional First Aid: Practical Strategies for Treating Failure, Rejection, Guilt and Other Everyday Psychological Injuries. "When it comes to attention and productivity, our brains have a finite amount," he says.

"It's like a pie chart, and whatever we're working on is going to take up the majority of that pie. There's not a lot left over for other things, with the exception of automatic behaviors like walking or chewing gum." Moving back and forth between several tasks actually wastes productivity, he says, because your attention is expanded on the act of switching gears—plus, you never get fully "in the zone" for either activity.

2. It's slowing you down

Contrary to popular belief, multitasking doesn't save time. In fact, it will probably take you longer to finish two projects when you're jumping back and forth than it would to finish each one separately. The same is true even for behaviors as seemingly automatic as driving: In a 2008 University of Utah study, drivers took longer to reach their destinations when they chatted on cell phones.

"What tends to save the most time is to do things in batches," says Winch. "Pay your bills all at once, then send your emails all at once. Each task requires a specific mindset, and once you get in a groove you should stay there and finish."

3. You're making mistakes

4. It's stressing you out

When University of California researchers measured the heart rates of employees with and without constant access to office email, they found that those who received a steady stream of messages stayed in a perpetual "high alert" mode with higher heart rates. Those without constant email access did less multitasking and were less stressed because of it.

And it's not only the physical act of multitasking that causes stress; it's the consequences, as well, says Winch. "If you do poorly on an exam because you studied while watching a baseball game on TV, that can certainly trigger a lot of stress—even self-esteem issues and depression."

5. You're missing out on life

Forget seeing the forest for the trees or the glass half full—people who are busy doing two things at once don't even see obvious things right in front of them, according to a 2009 study from Western Washington University.

Specifically, 75% of college students who walked across a campus square while talking on their cell phones did not notice a clown riding a unicycle nearby. The researchers call this "inattentional blindness," saying that even though the cell-phone talkers were technically looking at their surroundings, none of it was actually registering in their brains.

6. Your memory may suffer

It makes sense that if you try to do two things at once—read a book and watch television, for example—that you're going to miss important details of one or both. But even interrupting one task to suddenly focus on another can be enough to disrupt short term memory, according to a 2011 study.

When University of California San Francisco researchers asked participants to study one scene, but then abruptly switched to a different image, people ages 60 to 80 had a harder time than those in their 20s and 30s disengaging from the second picture and remembering details about the first. As the brain ages, researchers say, it has a harder time getting back on track after even a brief detour.

7. It's hurting your relationships

"This is an area where I think multitasking has a much bigger effect than most people realize," says Winch. "A couple is having a serious talk and the wife says 'Oh, let me just check this message.' Then the husband gets mad, and then he decides to check his messages, and communication just shuts down."

One recent study from the University of Essex even shows that just having a cell phone nearby during personal conversations—even if neither of you are using it—can cause friction and trust issues. "Do your relationship a favor and pay your partner some exclusive attention for 10 minutes," says Winch. "It can make a big difference."

8. It can make you overeat

Being distracted during mealtime can prevent your brain from fully processing what you've eaten, according to a 2013 review of 24 previous studies. Because of that, you won't feel as full, and may be tempted to keep eating—and to eat again a short time later.

Experts recommend that even people who eat alone should refrain from turning on the television while eating, and to truly pay attention to their food. Eating lunch at your computer? Slow down and take a break from the screen to focus on each bite.

9. You're not actually good at it

Yes, you. You may think you're a master multitasker, but, according to a 2013 University of Utah study, that probably means you're actually among the worst.

The research focused specifically on cell phone use behind the wheel, and it found that people who scored highest on multitasking tests do not frequently engage in simultaneous driving and cell-phone use—probably because they can better focus on one thing at a time. Those who do talk and drive regularly, however, scored worse on the tests, even though most described themselves as having above average multitasking skills.

10. It's dampening your creativity

Multitasking requires a lot of what's known as "working memory", or temporary brain storage, in layman's terms. And when working memory's all used up, it can take away from our ability to think creatively, according to research from the University of Illinois at Chicago.

"Too much focus can actually harm performance on creative problem-solving tasks".

11. You can't Only Handle its once

The problem with multitasking, though, is that it makes Only Handling It Once a near impossibility—instead, you're handling it five or six times, says Winch. "If you're going to stick to this principle, you need to be disciplined and plan out your day so that when a distraction arises or a brilliant idea occurs to you, you know that there will be time for it later."

12. It can be dangerous

Texting or talking on a cell phone even with a hands-free device, is as dangerous as driving drunk—yet that doesn't stop many adults from doing it, even while they have their own children in the car.

It's not just driving that puts you at risk for the consequences of multitasking, either. Research also shows that people who use mobile devices while walking are less likely to look before stepping into a crosswalk. And in one study, one in five teenagers who went to the emergency room after being hit by a car admitted they were using a smartphone at the time of the accident.

"Many people feel they must multi-task because everybody else is multitasking, but this is partly because they are all interrupting each other so much."

— Marilyn vos Savant

Principle of Time Management & Life Management

24. Strike a balance between Work & Life

You must strike a balance: that between work and home and outside interests and commitments. If you overdo the work, the other things—and they are important—suffer. What is more, damage, if damage is done, is insidious.

You may not be aware of a difficulty until it is too late and begins to cause some real problems. The answer is to consciously seek to strike a balance; indeed, you may want to lay down some rules for yourself about this, specifying maximum hours for work, travel, or spending on specific things.

*"If you want your children to turn out well, spend **twice as much time** with them and **half as much money**."*

—Abigail Van Buren

Time Management is a great way to better achieve Work-Life Balance

The answer to maximizing productivity in your job is not to work longer and longer hours. This may seem like a contradiction in terms. Surely if you put in more hours you will achieve more as a result?

Yes, perhaps to an extent you will.

The point, however, is that there are limits. The day is fixed at 24 hours for us all; the amount of time we have to work with is finite. It seems to be one of life's rules that jobs that are interesting are not compatible with a strictly 9–5 attitude; in part, this is probably why they are interesting, so I am not advocating this, though I do believe the long hours culture in some organizations has hit diminishing returns.

"Imagine life as a game in which you are juggling some five balls in the air. You name them — **work, family,**

health, friends and spirit and you're keeping all of these in the air. You will soon understand that work is a rubber ball. If you drop it, it will bounce back. But the other four balls — family, health, friends, and spirit — are made of glass. If you drop one of these, they will be irrevocably scuffed, marked, nicked, damaged, or even shattered. They will never be the same. You must understand that and strive for balance in your life."

Finding work-life balance is hugely important. You must be able to balance your career and your home life. It is important to understand how with time management, we can enjoy work-life balance.

1. Use Positive Affirmations

For centuries, we have been advised to have faith in the power of positive affirmations and should try our best to harness it. Positivity will change your quality of life and is the first of these methods for programming your subconscious mind is "positive self-talk," or the use of positive affirmations. Our subconscious mind is giant and have absolute power.

These are commands that you pass from your conscious mind to your subconscious mind. Positive affirmations are statements that you either say out loud or say to yourself with the emotion and enthusiasm that drives the words into your subconscious mind as new operating instructions.

Begin by repeating this positive affirmation over and over to yourself.

"I am excellent at time management! I am excellent at time management!"

Any command or positive affirmation repeated over and over again in a spirit of faith, acceptance, and belief, will eventually be accepted by your subconscious mind. One of my favorite time management affirmation is this:

"I use my time well. I use my time well. I use my time well."

You will then find that your external behaviors will start to reflect your internal programming to improve your work-life balance and quality of life.

2. Use Visualization To Program Your Subconscious Mind

Visualization is another powerful technique which you can use to program your subconscious. Mental pictures most immediately influence your subconscious mind. **In self-image psychology, the person you see is the person you will be through positive affirmations.**

> **Begin to see yourself as well organized, efficient and effective in time management.**

Recall and recreate memories and pictures of yourself when you were performing at your best. Think of a time when you were working efficiently and effectively, and getting through an enormous amount of work. Play this picture of yourself over and over again on the screen of your mind.

3. Relax, And Meditate

The third time management method is simple. First, you sit or lie in a quiet place where you can be completely alone in the silence. Through positive affirmations, imagine yourself going through an important upcoming experience, such as a meeting, a presentation, a negotiation or even a date that would improve your work-life balance and your quality of life.

As you sit or lie completely relaxed, create a picture of the coming event and see it unfolding perfectly in every respect. See yourself as calm, positive, happy and in complete control. See the other people doing and saying exactly what you would want them to do if the situation was perfect.

4. Imagine You Are Excellent At Time Management

The fourth mental technique is to imagine that you are already excellent at time management. Imagine that you have been selected for a role in a movie or stage play.

In this role, you are to act the part of a person who is extremely well organized in every respect. As you go through your daily life, imagine you are an actor who is playing this part, who is already very good at time management. Act as if you are already using your time efficiently and well.

Pretend that you are an expert in personal efficiency and time management. When you pretend that you are excellent in time management, eventually the action, which is under your direct control, will develop the mindset or the belief in your subconscious mind.

People resolve, over and over again, to get serious about time management by focusing, setting better priorities and overcoming procrastination. They intend to get serious about time management sometime, but unfortunately, "the road to hell is paved with good intentions."

Time Management Motivation

For you to develop sufficient desire to develop time management and organizational skills, you must be intensely motivated by the benefits you feel you will enjoy. You must want the results badly enough to overcome the natural inertia that keeps you doing things the same old way.

If everyone agrees that excellent time management is a desirable skill, why is it that so few people can be described as "well organized, effective and efficient?" Over the years, I have found that many people have ideas about time management that are simply not true.

Here Is The Key: Structure And Organize Everything That You Possibly Can.

Think ahead, plan for contingencies, prepare thoroughly, and focus on specific results. Only then can you be completely relaxed and spontaneous when the situation changes.

The better organized you are in the factors that are under your control, the greater freedom and flexibility you have to quickly make changes whenever they are necessary.

 *"You will never feel truly satisfied by work until you are satisfied by life."*

— **Heather Schuck**

Find inspiration — quotes, videos, audiobooks

"Your children get only one childhood. Make it memorable." —Regina Brett

Following a to-do list or a specific pattern can be boring. It's hard to concentrate at work when you aren't fully motivated within. Instead of wasting that time doing something unproductive, utilize it to inspire yourself.

Tape those cliched time-management quotes around your desk. Watch motivational or TEDx videos or listen to audiobooks talking about time management tips at work. Or, just go for a small walk.

We are familiar with the procrastination phenomena in which you either do nothing at all or engage in useless activities. The chronic procrastinators get an unusual high in putting important things for later and when it is too late, they start panicking. Don't let procrastination take over your life and let it become a part of your lifestyle.

The best way to deal with procrastination is to break your work into a number of tasks. It not only makes it doable but also gives you a starting point to begin work. Also, try making detailed timelines that give you an exact idea of deadlines. When you surround yourself with people who take action and crush goals instantly, you automatically imbibe such habits and become more proactive with work.

Toward the end of an excessive number of hours, productivity (and concentration) will drop. For those readers who are managers, remember that the overall work capacity of the team you control is very much greater than yours, so it always makes sense to take a team view of things rather than just opting to do more yourself.

Finally, excessively long hours worked can be misunderstood and make it appear to others that you are inefficient, which is presumably the reverse of how you want to appear.

Long hours will be necessary on some occasions, to complete a particular project, say, but in excess are likely to produce declining standards and run risks that make smarter working a much more attractive option. It is something to ponder (though not late into the night!) in order to make sure that you create a working pattern that is well balanced in this way.

> *"You don't have to make yourself miserable to be successful. It's natural to look back and mythologize the long nights and manic moments of genius, but success isn't about working hard, it's about working smart."*
>
> **— Andrew Wilkinson**

Principle of Time Management & Life Management

25  Rejuvenate Yourself, Recharge Your Life

"We must be willing to get rid of the life we've planned, so as to have the life that is waiting for us. The old skin has to be shed before the new one can come."

— **Joseph Campbell**

"Rest when you're weary. Refresh and renew yourself, your body, your mind, your spirit. Then get back to work."

— **Ralph Marston**

Unless we as individuals are operating at our highest possible energy levels, we simply have no ability to "recharge" or bring new life to our work.

It may sound counterintuitive, but breaks are one of the effective time management strategies. How? Let's assume two scenarios. In the first scenario, picture a team member working on a task for 5–7 hours at a stretch. And, another team member is working on the same task with frequent small breaks. Who do you think is using his time effectively? Of course, the later.

Smart time management isn't always about doing something or the other. It also emphasizes on the fact that little breaks after an hour or so can take your productivity to another level.

In today's hyper-connected world, it's easy to fall into the trap of being connected 24/7. We feel guilty during the weekend about not working ahead or completing an extra project. All the time our body and mind need rest to function properly. Taking time to recharge is crucial to sustaining motivation, passion, and productivity. Quick breaks during a stressful deadline can help you maintain focus, renew creativity, and make you feel more refreshed when you return to your task.

Consider the word rejuvenation:

Webster's definition is **"to make (someone) feel or look young, healthy, or energetic again;"** and **"to give new strength or energy to (something)."**

For longer periods of recharging, take regular work vacations of at least a week off throughout the year.

> **Bill Gates, for example, went into seclusion for one week twice a year to focus and plan. Many of Microsoft's innovation ideas came from those "Think Weeks".**

Schedule breaks throughout your day to help you recharge and take regular vacations throughout the year.

> **Rest is the best medicine for sustainable long-term productivity.**

> *"Life is not measured by the number of breaths we take, but by the moments that take our breath away."*
>
> — Maya Angelou

In today's hectic and very demanding world, we are often confronted with especially high levels of stress and pressure that can lead to exhaustion if not well managed. How wonderful it would be to truly rejuvenate ourselves—to feel young and healthy again, with a new strength and energy for both our business and families.

In the book The Power of Full Engagement, authors Jim Loehr and Tony Schwartz note that,

> **"We live in a world that celebrates work and activity, ignores renewal and recovery, and fails to recognize that both are necessary for sustained high performance."**

They suggest that when performing at our highest levels, we are drawing from four separate sources of energy—physical, emotional, mental, and spiritual—and we should be disciplined in the regular use and renewal of these energy sources. They suggest that if we manage these resources effectively, we can build the capacity to live a more productive, fully engaged life.

It is imperative to take time for regular personal renewal. Perhaps as a result of personal beliefs or societal dogma, we often think personal renewal is only for those who deserve it—an award for some achievement. The rest of us who are undeserving wear the hours worked every week like a badge of honor, boasting of our 70 or 80 hours at the office.

What would it look like in your life if you turned this around? What if instead of looking at the time for your personal rejuvenation as a reward for certain work accomplished, you see it as a key ingredient to be more effective and as the path to achieve significant improvement and results in your work?

We face many forces that compete for our time and energy. It's all too easy to fall into the trap of overworking to the point of exhaustion, rarely taking time for our own renewal. One of my habits at the beginning of each calendar year is to schedule blocks of renewal time over the entire year. Occasionally, I may need to adjust some of these dates, but when I have to take away from one of my scheduled renewal times, I simply move it to another date, instead of deleting it.

Another way I have found rejuvenation in my own life is through positive habits or rituals that provide a break from my work routine. My parents instilled many positive renewal rituals into my life that I continue to practice with my own family today. Growing up, we had regularly scheduled meals together as a family. Even my father, who was incredibly busy running his business, would take a break each evening for the family meal. If there was more work to be done, he would go back out to office after dinner, but he would religiously spend this time with us. Sunday was set aside as a day of rest, and my parents had strict rules for the type of activities allowed in order to provide the optimal amount of rest and renewal for the week ahead. Though I sometimes fought those boundaries as a child, I now look back and recognize what a gift they were. We also took at least one week every year for a family vacation, and all family members participated. By continuing to follow rituals such as these, I have found it naturally creates a time of renewal that I would not sacrifice.

Taking the time for rejuvenation is key to be more effective leadership. We certainly want to bring our best selves to work. When we are fresh and operating with peak energy, we create a positive environment for our team, where they too can flourish. We approach work with renewed vigor and creativity. Others see our renewed passion—and this passion is electric and contagious. Imagine the ripple effect we could have on our team when we showed up with this ideal level of energy and enthusiasm. Imagine what we could accomplish if others followed our example—improving results, increasing morale, even having fun at work!

Commit to scheduling regular time for rejuvenation. By faithfully renewing our physical, emotional, mental, and spiritual selves, we will develop increased energy for our work, our team, and our families. The result is the capacity to live more highly engaged and truly satisfying lives.

"We must always change, renew, rejuvenate ourselves; otherwise, we harden."

— **Johann Wolfgang von Goethe**

Self-Care Techniques To Rejuvenate And Restore Yourself

1. Follow the life Mantra of Attachment & Detachment.
2. Schedule time for a divine self care ritual in the morning and evening. Rituals can include exercising, meditating, reading, writing, looking at your vision board, or saying affirmations.
3. Set aside 5-10 minutes of uninterrupted time to practice daily prayer and gratitude.
4. Awake the Child within yourself.
5. Pick up any sport you like, and on weekly basis, ensure you play your favourite sport.
6. Give your fun time. If you like music, learn to play any musical instrument. This is best stress buster.

7. Turn technology off, don't try and multi-task, just enjoy your meal.
8. Declutter your home, office, and car. Get rid of anything that doesn't make your life easier or more beautiful.
9. Practice extreme self-care weekly as a non-negotiable. Have a checklist with your favourite self-care practices and tick them off as you complete them throughout the week.
10. Start work late from time to time.
11. Finish work early from time to time.
12. Practice daily meditation and/or yoga.
13. Schedule lunch out with a friend once a week.
14. Take time out to design your life just the way you want it.
15. Find an exercise that you thoroughly enjoy and do it several times a week.
16. Surround yourself with other supportive and growing people.
17. Say "no" to more things.
18. Do one thing every week that scares you. Challenge and grow yourself—you'll feel better as a person and your confidence will soar.
19. Take time out every evening to reflect on the day—what worked, what didn't work, what will you do differently tomorrow?
20. Drink water every single day.
21. Turn off your computer and your phone every night by a certain time. No peeking!
22. Start your day with warm water and lemon.
23. Create a list of activities that are fun and exciting. Commit to doing 2-3 every weekend.
24. Schedule in your self-care at the start of the week. Commit to your schedule.
25. Schedule two-week or month-long holidays throughout the year, just because.

26. Eliminate tasks that drain your energy (delegate or delete them).
27. Don't respond to emails right away, take your time on the emails that need a proper response. Think them through.
28. Focus on achieving in all areas of your life, not just in your business or career. When was the last time you paid attention to fun, your health, romance with your partner, friends, or spiritual development?
29. Take yourself to the park to read an amazing book and enjoy some fresh air.
30. Buy yourself something amazing after accomplishing something amazing.

Principle of Time Management & Life Management
On Things That Don't Matter, Don't spend much time in making decision – Be real Quick

"Time = Life"

"Therefore, waste your time and waste your life, or master your time and master your life."

— Alan Lakein

We make hundreds of small, medium, and big decisions every day. 90% of the decisions we make don't matter. Success comes from identifying and focusing your energy on the 10%.

Small decisions impact you for a day, such as what to wear or where to eat. Medium impact your life for a year, such as deciding to go back to school or rent a different room. In the long term though, very few decisions matter. Those are the big decisions: they are worthy of serious pondering, discussion, investigation, investment, and decision making.

Invest your focus on big decisions and make quick calls on medium and small decisions.

In **"10–10–10: A Life-Transforming Idea"**, Suzy Welch introduces a simple decision-making system. When you have a decision to make, ask yourself the following three questions:

➢ Question 1 - How will I feel about this decision 10 minutes from now?

➢ Question 2 - How will I feel about it 10 months from now?

➢ Question 3 - And in 10 years from now?

Successful people don't spend a lot of time pondering over small and medium decisions. A great time management technique is to train yourself to be quick when making them as well.

"Take care of the minutes and the hours will take care of themselves."

— Lord Chesterfield

On an average, Indian adult makes 35,000 decisions every day. That number may sound extreme but, think about how many decisions you make just before starting work each morning. You decide if you should eat breakfast, what to eat, what shirt to wear, what shoes, what pants, likely read some emails that you had to think about...the list goes on and on, and that's just basic things that don't compare to what you have to think about at work.

The more decisions you make, the less mental capacity you have.

There are two ways to reduce the number of decisions you make:

➢ Stop making decisions that don't generate value. For example, choices like what you eat for breakfast or which color shirt you wear have a negligible impact and aren't worth the effort. Instead, choose a routine breakfast and wardrobe so, in the mornings, you can grab and go. This practice has been used by highly productive people like Steve Jobs and Mark Zuckerberg who wore similar outfits every day. Make a list of all your decisions like these and take actions to reduce the frequency that you make them.

➢ Delegate decisions that don't require your direct input. If you're a higher level professional, you probably make a lot of administrative decisions that aren't worth your time and energy. Delegate tasks such as scheduling, database management and other process-oriented tasks to assistants who can quickly take care of them.

"To think too long about doing a thing often becomes its undoing."

— Eva Young

		Principle of Time Management & Life Management
		## Commute Time is Your Think Time
Time is valuable only when you add value to it

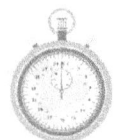

"There's only one thing more precious than our time and that's who we spend it on."

— Leo Christopher

Make most of your commuting time – Think Time

Every successful person wishes to complete most of the useful tasks in 24 hours. His whole routine centres around the best use of time. As Myke Merdoc has rightly said, 'The secret of your future is hidden in your daily routine.'

> Travelling is an important art of your daily routine. Nowadays every person has to travel a lot and travelling takes up a lot of time. The only difference is that an ordinary person sits idle during his journey whereas a successful person makes maximum use of this time.

Mahatma Gandhi used to take a good nap to get refreshed during his travels. When Napoleon had to travel with his army during the war, he utilised his time by writing letters. Edison was so conscious of utilising his travel time that during his adolescence age whenever he travelled by train, he remained busy doing his experiments. The founder of Microsoft, Bill Gates, too applies this principle by doing all his urgent conversations on this mobile while travelling.

All the successful people remain conscious about the utilisation of time because they know that time is the most powerful thing in the world and success is possible only through the best utilisation of time.

We can also take advantage of our travel time. The people who have jobs have to spend a lot of time in travelling from office to home and vice versa. In case of the salesmen, most of their time gets wasted in travelling only. We must know that if we travel for two and a half hours daily, it means 10% time of our life is being spent on travel alone. During this time, you can do some significant work and make best use of your time.

We have a lot of downtime throughout our days: commuting, lines, waiting rooms, in-between tasks, small breaks in the schedule, etc. If we add all this time up, we have around 1–3 hours of "gap time" every day. Be as strategic about your breaks as you are about your day in general. While these short periods might not be enough to do Deep Work, we can still work on little things that contribute to your work, development, and growth.

Let us start using our think time to increase our available time and reduce stress. Important is to understand what is our think time.

When you have nothing to active to do like when travelling, while shaving, when getting up etc etc, this is your think time. Personally, I find it a good way of reducing stress.

Use your Think Time

Mentally, we need to list down what is crowding our mind. You may also write it down. Then you need to make mental calculations to see more clearly what you can do and what you can not do. We all have a go and a no-go device – like quality control department has – in our mind which tells us what will give us happiness and what will give us stress. We need to find out how much of each is involved, and then superimpose our extraneous factors on the stress giving activities – such as pressures from spouse, children, colleagues, friends and relatives. Again, in stress-related activities, we need to calculate how much trade-off is possible, and we need to try to reduce stress damage as much as possible.

I manage to squeeze out several think times during the day, including my sleeping time – I use unbelievable power of my subconscious mind. Earlier, I used to spend 60 mins to 120 mins tossing in my bed; now I fall asleep sometimes in as little as 10 mins. I keep my mind uncluttered and decongested of whatever I do not need. I want to meet my needs and not my greed. At night, before sleeping, we empty our pockets and put things away. I empty my mind several times a day of whatever I do not need and of things said by others that hurt me at the time or may hurt me later.

Use "gap time" effectively to develop new skills, strategic planning, and personal growth.

By taking advantage of your downtime, you end up getting more done and having more free time for fun after work. It really makes me amaze that many people with long commutes do not use the time in any manner. Even if you are driving there are great ways to use the time.

Audio books are a great way to learn something new while driving. When I had a long commute, I used to listen to 3-5 audio books a week. These days there are many easy ways to bring great audio with you. You can rent books on CD, or you can download audiobooks or podcasts to your iPod.

"A man who dares to waste one hour of life has not discovered the value of life." — Charles Darwin

If you commute by train or bus, you really do not have an excuse for not utilizing the time. However, next time you are on the train, take the time to observe other passengers. How many are doing anything productive? If you ride the train you can read or even write. You can do work while en-route your destination.

Time Shift to Save Time

One of the best ways to same time is manage your commute is to avoid the rush. If everyone else is driving to work at 8.30 am, what if you left at 8 am? Would it cut your commute in half? For some people it does. Time shifting, or moving tasks to more opportune times, can save you considerably over the long run. I know some co-workers who minimize their commute time by coming in at 8 am and leaving at 5 pm. Some companies not only support this type of schedule, they actively encourage it.

Skip the Commute Sometimes

Another great way to minimize commute time is to skip it from time-to-time. If your employer supports it, look at a partial work from home arrangement. During Covid-19, many organisation started work from home culture. Indeed, many of organisation is using WFM as an effective tool for productivity enhancement as well as better time management. In today's telecommuting world, more and more employers are doing this. A word of caution, only do this if you can actually work from home. If you do not have the proper environment or discipline, you are asking for trouble.

Time spent in commuting can be analysed. Whether you travel by car or by train, ask yourself such questions as:

- How much time have I spent commuting during the past few months?
- What are the gains from it?
- Are the benefits of commuting worth the time invested in terms of the accomplishments and lifestyle I want most?
- If not, what are the alternatives? Do I have any real choice?
- If commuting is the only answer, am I making best use of my commuting time? When travelling could I:
    - ✓ read more?
    - ✓ listen to tape recordings?
    - ✓ do some paperwork?
    - ✓ plan or analyse problems?
    - ✓ make phone calls?
    - ✓ do some keep-fit exercises?
    - ✓ do some memory tests;
    - ✓ learn a foreign language?
    - ✓ update foreign-language skills?
    - ✓ send e-mail and faxes from my laptop computer?
    - ✓ do research on the internet?
    - ✓ check out useful websites?

> Would the benefits of first-class travel outweigh the extra cost?
> Where flexitime is available, have I chosen my travel times to the best overall advantage?

 "It is the time you have wasted for your rose that makes your rose so important."

— Antoine de Saint-Exupéry

Use Commute time as Think Time or Learning Time

1. Look into Carpooling or Using Public Transportation

This might sound counter-productive to saving time instead of driving to work by yourself, but those extra few minutes spent on carpooling actually helps you utilize the whole chunk of commuting time better for the productive hacks mentioned here. Plus, you get to network with people from different fields and contribute to the environment by saving fuel. Use apps like Waze Carpool and Uber pool for a hassle-free service.

2. Use The Time to Sort Out Your Thoughts

Usually, our mornings are a blur of rushed activities – there's hardly any time to pause and breathe. Use the time spent commuting to gather your scattered thoughts so you can start the day with a centralized focus. You can also plan out minute details regarding the project you've been working on, or any hustle you might be engaged in (shout out to the over-achieving go-getters of the world!). Take the time to deliberate about things often helps create solutions to complicated problems you might be dealing with for some time.

3. Plan The Day Ahead

With your thoughts and ideas sorted (or if you're already the sorted-out type), you can now move on to plan the day before you start it. Almost all successful people in this world start their day with a clear plan in mind and on their workbooks because it helps them get more done within the day. Isn't that what's productivity all about? Doing this on the commute helps you get straight to work when you reach the office. Use apps like Evernote to make to-do lists and to keep journals. You can also use its voice note option to dictate your tasks into it if you're driving or riding.

4. Listen to Self-Improvement Podcasts and Audiobooks

It's ideal to start a day on a positive note to get the maximum productivity out of yourself. If you haven't already done this after waking up in the morning, now is a good time. Listening to audiobooks is, of course, not the only option for people walking, driving, or riding to work. However, drivers should be extra cautious even when listening to audiobooks.

5. Preplan the Phone Calls That You Can Make During Your Commute

Get casual and regular phone calls to friends and family out of the way during this time of the day. It will be a task off the to-do list for the day, however insignificant it might be. You can also set up a telephonic meeting at this time, but make sure you're not in a very noisy place.

6. Schedule an Online Course

Take your commuting productivity to the next level by taking an online course. However, this only works for those who spend a good amount of uninterrupted time on the move, because you really need to be attentive or you won't learn anything at all. Taking a half-hour class each day for a month can teach you a new skill!

7. Learn a New Skill / Language

If an online course sounds too ambitious to you, learning a language is a much simpler alternative. Knowing more than one language is, for many jobs, important and helpful if you're a travel junkie (which most of us seem to be these days). Duolingo is a very efficient app that takes you from zero to sixty in simple and easy-to-master techniques.

Alternatively, you can also use this time to do things that make you feel guilty of doing because they eat into your work hours, like social media or makeup tutorials by your favorite Youtuber.

Remember, time is valuable only when you add value to it.

 *"The two most powerful warriors are patience and time."*

— Leo Tolstoy

Similarly, don't miss to take advantage of waiting times.

It happens to everyone: we wait in lines, waiting rooms, airport terminals, train stations, etc.

> Answer emails on your phone, catch up on missed phone calls, stretch/exercise, relax or meditate. Carry a book/Kindle with you and read. Listen to podcasts on your phone.

Don't let unexpected queues catch you unprepared.

People sometimes ask me, "With such a filled life, where do you find time to read all the books you read?" Here's the answer. I leverage "waiting time"—and I've been doing so for years now.

> **"Waiting time" is the time I spend waiting for something, someone or to get somewhere.**
>
> For instance, when I bring my car to the shop for an oil change or for repairs, I have to wait for the job on the car to get done. I have to choose what I'll do with that "waiting time". I can sit passively and stargaze like an owl at night, waiting for my car to be ready, or I can plunge my eyes into a good book while I wait. I opt for the book.

I do the same when I have to commute by Metro. At a time in my life, my commute was about 2.5 hours a day. You can get a lot of reading (and writing) done during this time.

I do the same when I'm driving somewhere—except for the writing part, of course! My driving time is "learning time". Mainly, I listen to inspirational and educational podcasts or other audio material. Side note, when my kids are in the car, they hijack my sounds system: we listen to music…

Instead of simply letting "waiting time" past by, I much rather invest it doing something I deem productive, such as reading a book that can potentially change my life or writing a post that can serve someone.

The point is: Don't let your "waiting time" slip away but use it productively. You have to wait anyway. Why not make the best use of this time?

If you take an account of all the time you spend waiting, you'll realize how much time you can leverage to do things that are important to you. You can add 2 or 3 productive hours to your day simply by leveraging your "waiting time" better.

Because reading and writing are important to me, I leverage as many "waiting time" as I can to read and write. And this translates in reading many books and writing thousands of words a year; those short burst of time add up.

Perhaps, you're not into reading and writing. Find what works for you. How can you use your "waiting time" in a way that adds value to your life? Perhaps, you can plan, brainstorm, or listen to podcasts.

By leveraging "waiting time" you can transform that time—which for most is "wasted time"—into productive time.

 28 	Principle of Time Management & Life Management
	Eliminate Distractions

"You will never reach your destination if you stop and throw stones at every dog that barks."
— Winston S. Churchill

In Today's world, Distractions barks on us from every corner.

Distractions hurt your productivity and focus.

A study from the University of California Irvine found that it takes an average of 23 minutes and 15 seconds to get back to the task after getting distracted. Best-selling author Gary Keller illustrated in "The ONE Thing: The Surprisingly Simple Truth Behind Extraordinary Results" what happens when you get interrupted:

When you lose your focus, it can take you twice as long to get back into the groove.

> Half an hour completely focused on a task is more productive than 2 hours switching between tasks.

Time Management is Life Management

Eliminate distractions from your work to avoid task switching costs.
- Turn off all notifications on your phone, computer, and tablet
- Leave your phone in odd places that prevent you from immediately finding it
- Work with headphones as people are less likely to approach you with a non-urgent question or gossip if you look plugged in and on-task
- If you find interesting articles, save them to Pocket or Instapaper to read later, such as during the commute
- The internet is a distracting place. Turn-off your Wi-Fi when your tasks don't require internet connectivity
- Don't browse social media at work at all. If you can't resist, designate "distraction time" and browse it for a couple of minutes. Take out of social media exactly what you want
- Use "Do Not Disturb" functions on chat systems
- Similarly, use Inbox Pause to stop getting flooded with new emails. Turn-off Pop window for every new mail to your mail-box.

"Meditation puts distractions in quarantine."

— **Khang Kijarro Nguyen**

Your time may be impacted by external factors imposed by other people and things. You can decrease or eliminate time spent in these activities by implementing some simple tips listed below.

Telephone
- Use voice mail and set aside time to return calls.
- Avoid long talk. Stay focused on the reason for the call.
- Stand up while you talk on the phone. You are more likely to keep the conversation brief.
- Take any necessary action immediately following the call.
- Set aside times of the day for receiving calls and let others know when you are available.
- Keep phone numbers readily available near the telephone.

Unexpected Visitors

- Establish blocks of time when you are available for visits.
- Tell the visitor politely that you cannot meet with them at this time and schedule the visit for a more convenient time.
- Set a mutually agreeable time limit for the visit.
- When someone comes to the door, stand up and have your meeting standing.

Meetings

- Know the purpose of the meeting in advance.
- Arrive on time.
- Start and finish the meeting on time.
- Prepare an agenda and stick to it. Use a timed agenda, if necessary.
- Don't schedule meetings unless they are necessary and have a specific purpose or agenda.

Mail and E-mail

- Set aside a specific time to view and respond to your mail and e-mail, but don't let it accumulate to the point that it becomes overwhelming to sort.
- Turn off instant messaging features on e-mail.
- Handle each item only once, if possible. Practice the options for dealing with clutter listed earlier.
- Sort mail near a garbage can and delete junk e-mail immediately from your electronic mailbox.
- Answer written messages by responding on the margins or bottom of the page.

Family Obligations

- Establish a master calendar for each family member to post their time commitments.
- Make each family member responsible for consulting the master calendar for potential conflicts.
- Create a central area for posting communications such as appointment reminders, announcements, and messages.

"Don't get sidetracked by people who are not on track."

We've all been there. Even with the best of intentions to stay on task, we still catch ourselves scrolling through social media when we should be working on a project. We can't help but grab our cell phone the moment we hear a notification. And then there's email! If we aren't checking it every five minutes, we worry we might miss something important.

Distractions can seem impossible to avoid. Statistics show that distractions cause a massive loss in productivity. The typical manager is interrupted every eight minutes, and employees generally spend 28 percent of their time dealing with unnecessary interruptions and trying to get back on track.

It is important to take back control of our time and attention. Below are proven strategies for overcoming distractions and reclaiming your focus.

1. Put yourself in distraction-free mode.

Begin building habits that help you eliminate distractions and stay focused. Start by creating an environment in which you're less tempted to get preoccupied with something other than what you're working on. This isn't always easy to do. For one, many of us rely on a computer to do our work, but we also find our biggest distractions enabled by the use of a computer on the internet. If you constantly find yourself wandering over to video or shopping websites, try using a website blocker app.

Work to create habits that signal to yourself and those around you that you're in distraction-free mode. Close the door of your office. Put on noise-cancelling headphones. Turn off your phone or put it on silent and move it away from you (so you can't easily pick it up). If you work in an open office, you may find it helpful to move to a quieter location. Studies have found that distractions happen 64 percent more often in an open office, and we're interrupted by others more often in that environment as well.

Remove as many excuses and distractions as you can so you can bring your full attention to one task at a time -- no multitasking.

2. Set three main objectives every day.

A long list of things to do can feel insurmountable and leave us feeling overwhelmed. We're ready to give up before we start, and that's when it becomes easy to give in to distractions. You can offset this by giving yourself 3 objectives to accomplish every day. Write them on a sticky note and post it where you can see it every time you look up from your work.

By limiting the number of daily goals, you'll have clearly defined what you need to work on. You'll work with greater intention on those tasks and your mind will be less apt to stray.

Ask yourself every morning: What are the three most important things to accomplish today? Any other tasks should be put on a separate to-do list. You can begin to tackle those less-important tasks once you've accomplished the first 3 goals.

3. Give yourself a shorter time frame.

More hours worked doesn't mean you necessarily get more things accomplished.

Parkinson's law says that "work tends to expand to fill the time we have available for its completion." And the thing is, we usually fill any time remaining with distractions. This is because our mind is wired to conserve energy whenever possible. If we don't have to do something, there's a good chance we won't do it. Instead, we'll allow ourselves to get sucked into a YouTube video or a game app on our phone.

On the other hand, when we're up against a deadline, we suddenly develop a laser-like focus and avoid distractions at all costs. When you know you have to get something done, you'll figure out a way to do it.

To eliminate distractions, give yourself a shorter time frame to finish your work. This is like giving yourself an artificial deadline, but backed up with something that holds you accountable. Tell your boss or client that you'll give them a draft of a project by the end of the day. Find an accountability partner who will hold you to your target time frame. However you do it, setting a hard deadline will help you avoid distractions and increase your productivity.

4. Monitor your mind wandering.

We spend nearly 50 percent of our waking time thinking about something other than what we're supposed to be doing, according to one Harvard study. We are on autopilot, and our mind is wandering, in part to avoid the effort of focusing on something. The key to heightened productivity is to notice when your mind is distracted and bring your attention back on task.

This means paying attention to your thoughts and recognizing when your mind starts drifting. This allows you to manage what you focus on and redirect your thoughts when you slip up. Instead of allowing yourself to keep meandering over to social media to check out your newsfeed, you actively put the brakes on this distraction.

Pay attention to what distractions are particularly hard to avoid, so you can catch them sooner. When you feel a desire to give in to a distraction, take a breath and purposely choose not to react to it. Once you've given in and allowed yourself to focus on something else, like reading emails, it's harder to regroup and bring your attention back to the task at hand.

In short, be mindful of your thoughts, instead of allowing yourself to skip between task and distraction.

5. Train your brain by making a game out of it.

Your mind is like a muscle. In order to use it effectively, you need to build it up. We need to train our brains to stay focused by gradually working on our concentration. This will strengthen our ability to focus for longer periods of time.

A great way to begin doing this is through the "Pomodoro Method", in which you set a timer and are completely focused on a task for a period of time, such as 45 minutes straight. Then allow yourself a 15-minute break.

If 45 minutes is a stretch, start with something more manageable, such as 25 minutes, and then give yourself a five-minute break.

The idea is to make a game of it -- challenge yourself to work diligently on your task until the timer rings. Then allow yourself to gorge on whatever distraction you want, but only for an allotted time.

After the break, it's back to work again until the timer rings. You'll be amazed by how much you can get done using this method!

6. Take on more challenging work.

If you're having trouble focusing and are chronically distracted, it may be that your work isn't engaging you fully. You might feel like you're working hard all day, but it could be that your mind is fighting boredom and looking to fill the time with something more interesting.

Complex tasks demand more of our working memory and attention, meaning we have less mental capacity remaining to wander to the nearest stimulating distraction. We're most likely to enter into a state of total work immersion when our abilities are challenged. We get bored when our skills greatly exceed the demands of our work -- such as when we do mindless data entry for several hours.

Assess the level of unproductive busywork you're doing. Are you having a hard time becoming engaged in the project? This could indicate that you have the capacity to take on more challenging projects. When we take on more complex work that pushes our skill and intellectual limits, we can become consumed and hyper-focused on the task. Our minds are wired to focus on anything that's novel, pleasurable or threatening. And tackling these tasks gives us a sense of achievement.

We have no such sense of accomplishment with a task we deem menial.

7. Break the cycle of stress and distraction.

Stress can also play a major role in our inability to focus or overcome distractions. Too often, we find ourselves trying to work while feeling overwhelmed. This leaves us frazzled and exhausted, easily distracted and unable to focus. If you're easily distracted, it can indicate that you're under elevated stress.

There's even a name for it: "easily distracted anxiety." Symptoms include:
- You have difficulty concentrating and your mind constantly drifts from what you were focusing on.
- You have more difficulty forming thoughts and staying on track than normal.
- Your thinking feels muddled and impaired.
- You feel your short-term memory isn't as good as it normally is.

Bringing your stress under control will help you regain your focus and overcome distractions more easily. You must find ways to calm your mind and relax your body to reduce the body's stress response. Make sure you get enough sleep. Practice breathing exercises and find ways to control your anxiety.

Principle of Time Management & Life Management

29. Use Technology for our Disposal

Don't become Slave of Technology

The IT revolution has changed our lives and work practice and continues to do so. Much that can be done is helpful: email is overwhelmingly helpful, not least to time management—though it has its dangers. There is much more, however, and the trick is finding what helps you.

Plethora of Technological assistance available for our Disposal.

Resolve to keep an eye on technological developments as they occur, spot and try anything that might help, and adopt anything that can be an ongoing help, making it current practice.

Every day, people introduce more and more technology to save your time. This technology, whether created for the home or office or even for use on the road, can put minutes and even hours back into each day. Few of helpful technological tools which can help in time management.

1. Handheld Digital Voice Recorders

You generate new ideas daily to improve your department, increase your service or sales, or help your subordinates. With a handheld digital voice recorder, you can record numerous messages and save them in folders for use now or later. These units are very versatile and in reasonable cost with a number of features.

They're also effective for dictating letters and other business correspondence. After you have your voice in this digital format, the options are endless: e-mail the file, upload it, post it, and edit it.

Many recorders come with additional accessories, such as docking stations so you're always charged and ready to go.

2. Phone Recording, Web Conferencing

Some phone conference services even offer you the feature of recording the calls. This allows you to upload the call to your intranet site and allow all the people in your organization to hear the training or strategy session.

Beyond the telephone bridge line level, an explosion of technology in Web conferencing solutions can enhance your presentations, sales, and meetings.

Web presentations are designed to be more interactive. You can take polling questions, break off in chat rooms, or allow participants to ask instant questions. The participants can also see a PowerPoint presentation just as if they were in a seminar or live program. The advantage is that both the presenters and listeners can do all this from the comfort of their own homes in their slippers and bathrobes (provided, of course, that they aren't using videoconferencing features at the time).

3. Wireless Headsets

If you're on the phone a lot, wireless headsets are a phenomenal advancement in technology that can save you hours a day. You don't even have to hold the receiver — your hands are free to flip through documents, take notes, or do whatever else helps you get your work done. You also don't have to be tied to your desk. You can walk around your office to clear your thinking and increase your focus. You can go down the hall to get a drink of water, all the while negotiating your big deal. At home, you can be cooking dinner, doing the laundry, or dusting while you're catching up with an old friend.

4. Mobile Phones and Text Messaging

Although the telephone isn't a brand new technology, you can always find improvements in speed, cost, and expansion options with the telephone. With the advancement of mobile technology, people are rarely out of touch. You can effectively reach anyone in the world at any time with a few punches of the buttons. (Unfortunately, the reverse is also true: You can be interrupted more easily.)

Mobile phones also give you the ability to text a quick message to get through to someone, which can save time or simply give you another avenue to communicate. If someone isn't returning your call, try texting a message to save you the time of making more calls.

5. Instant Messaging

To be able to send a quick note or delegate a quick, easy item instantly is tremendous. Instant messaging is really effective when you have colleagues who work in different locations. At my companies, I have multiple offices and employees in four time zones. Being able to instant message instead of picking up the phone and incurring long-distance charges is invaluable.

As handy as instant messaging can be, it can also be a huge source of distraction, leaving you with less time on your hands and less productivity if you don't keep it under wraps. Be sure to turn off your instant message when you really need to focus. The sound of a new message can drive you to distraction. That flashing toolbar compels most people to stop what they're doing and see what the sender wants.

6. E-book Readers

I love electronic book readers. I can carry 160 books in something the size of a gift book. It saves my time deciding which book to take with me on the road — I can take them all. When I feel like reading something light, I can. When I want to read the Gita, a business book, a relationship book, or a self-help book, I can do it with ease.

7. GPS Navigation Systems

One of the best new technologies for people who travel around town or even long distances is global positioning system (GPS) navigation. It can save you hours in trying to find that pesky address that doesn't appear on the old map. It also saves you the time and cost of looking up and printing out pages of directions from an Internet site.

You can even make midcourse corrections when you take a wrong turn. The soft computer voice tells you something like, "Recalculating route. Make a U-turn in 0.5 KM." It beats pulling into the nearest Petrol Pump station and trying to get directions from someone who may be as confused as you are.

8. Digital Video Recorders

Although television is a waste of time in many cases, most people have at least a few shows that they enjoy. If you have a digital video recorder (DVR), you'll never miss the shows you really want to watch. Better yet, by approaching your TV watching with intention and by setting beginning and ending times, you aren't as likely to get trapped in the mindless approach to watching TV, where you're tempted to channel surf or continue watching after your show has ended.

The other advantage is that you can skip every commercial in the program and dramatically reduce the time to view a show. An hour-long show often cuts down to less than 40 minutes. That's a time savings of 33 percent just for commercial zapping.

Principle of Time Management & Life Management
  Focus on your Physical & Mental Health

 *"To keep the body in good health is a duty... otherwise we shall not be able to keep the mind strong and clear."*

— Buddha

Scheduling time to relax can help you rejuvenate both physically and mentally.

The care and attention you give yourself is an important investment of time. Scheduling time to relax, or do nothing, can help you rejuvenate both physically and mentally, enabling you to accomplish tasks more quickly and easily. Learn to manage time according to your biological clock by scheduling priority tasks during your peak time of day, the time your energy level and concentration are at their best.

> **Poor time management can result in fatigue, moodiness, and more frequent illness. To reduce stress, you should reward yourself for a time management success. Take time to recognize that you have accomplished a major task or challenge before moving on to the next activity.**

Regardless of the time management strategies you use, you should take time to evaluate how they have worked for you. Ask yourself a few simple questions: Do you have a healthy balance between work and home life? Are you accomplishing the tasks that are most important in your life? Are you investing enough time in your own personal wellbeing?

If the answer is "no" to any of these questions, then reconsider your time management strategies and select ones that work better for you. Remember that successful time management today can result in greater personal happiness, greater accomplishments at home and at work, increased productivity, and a more satisfying future.

"If you know the art of deep breathing, you have the strength, wisdom and courage of ten tigers."

— **Chinese adage**

Sleep is a detrimental factor that could affect many things both positively and negatively. When you get a sound sleep for six to eight hours, not only you feel fresh and rejuvenated but it also contributes to a healthy lifestyle. On the contrary, when you don't get enough sleep, you are also increasing disease risks such as diabetes, obstructive sleep, obesity and more.

Human mind and body make better decisions and perform more efficiently when they are well-rested. You can decide quickly what to do, when and how. Develop a schedule for your sleep and stick to it every day. Try going to bed and waking up at the same time. There are many applications such as Calm, Sleep Cycle that tracks your sleeping patterns, help you get a sound sleep, and wakes you up as a more focused individual.

Sole Purpose of Life is to be Happy.

Happiness Mantra 6 – Don't fill your subconscious mind with all sorts of garbage

Your subconscious mind is a big store house for your conscious mind. Whatever you see, hear, think, feel and experience are all stored here as permanent memory. But, the problematic part is that, along with our thoughts and sense impressions, we are also throwing lot of emotional garbage and negativity (e.g. hatred, revenge, fear, anger, jealousy etc.) which is playing a real havoc here. Some people are constantly all the time even without being aware of it. Every time you think negative, it immediately gets fed into your subconscious mind. Whether you know about it or not, makes no difference in its effect.

Now the law is, whatever you have fed into your subconscious mind, it gives back the same to you. So, all the negative impressions and emotions filled here, jump back and create ripples in conscious mind in the form of impulses, urges, and passions and keep it restless. The horrible dreams you see in the night are the result of this negative, careless and thoughtless programming of subconscious mind.

Now what is the way out? You must begin immediately feeding the subconscious mind with strong and positive thoughts and emotions. This will gradually destroy negativities and impurities filled in the subconscious mind. Remember, Positive always overcomes negative. For this, your conscious mind will have to be watchful and alert for each thought which it is thinking and should only allow positive thoughts to enter.

To accomplish this, you will have to develop positive attitude towards everything, every event, every problem, every adversity and every misfortune by looking for hidden lessons and good in these things.

Further, control your reactions and limit your attachment towards various worldly things and situations. The stronger your reaction and attachments towards a certain thing, the stronger are the impressions created in your subconscious mind and the stronger the impressions, the stronger is the turbulence generated in your conscious mind. In fact, it is our reactions not the actions which are the root cause of our trouble.

> **Conscious mind is like a watchman or a gatekeeper. Subconscious mind is like a store. If the watchman is sleeping, anything can enter in the store. But, if the watchman is alert, he may regulate the entry by allowing only the right set of people and material in the store.**

"I find so many people struggling, often working harder, simply because they cling to old ideas. They want things to be the way they were; they resist change. Old ideas are their biggest liability. It is a liability simply because they fail to realize that while that idea or way of doing something was an asset yesterday, yesterday is gone."

— **Robert Kiyosaki**

Time Management Secrets

1. Admit the fact that we can not manage time, we can only manage ourself.

There are 24 hours in each day. You can't change that. As long as you focus on managing time - searching for systems, lists, and tools - you are ignoring the real issue: how to manage yourself.

2. Don't be a victim of Time mismanagement. Don't say "Too much to do" and "Not enough time".

Every time you repeat those words, you are letting yourself off the hook for managing yourself. You are blaming circumstances beyond your control and subscribing to victimhood. Of course, there is too much to do! Of course, there is not enough time! Get used to it!

3. Please understand clearly when you have too many priorities, it means you don't have any priority.

You can not have too many priorities. By definition, Priorities are those top few tasks that deserve attention next. If you have too many, you have none. You have to know your top few priorities at any time.

4. More is Less in Time Management - The more priorities we have, the less we will accomplish.

If you have 2-3 priorities, you will complete 2-3 tasks. If you have 4-10, you will complete 1-2. If you have more than 10, you will complete none. The more items on your list, the more time you spend messing with the list, jumping from task to task, and feeling paralyzed by indecision.

5. Most people carries crazy to-do lists most of the time. Be watchful for your To-Do List.

Pull all your lists together. Then try estimating the time needed to accomplish all of those tasks. What are the chances that the total exceeds all available time? Even if you shrink the numbers, convinced that you will suddenly be faster and more focused than ever, I bet the total exceeds the hours in a day.

6. Your to-do lists are incomplete.

Not only are your lists crazy long, they are incomplete. Think about it. Have you included enough time for meetings, email, and phone calls? Questions from customers and staff? Time to sleep, eat, exercise, relax, and call your mother? What about time to search for everything from people to passwords? Or rebooting, correcting credit card expiration dates, and sitting on hold? Everything. Now how do those total hours look? And what are the chances you've anticipated everything likely to pop up? Face it, there are not enough hours in a day!

7. Better to admit and understand, we can not finish everything.

As long as you believe you can - or need to! - finish everything, you will be frustrated and ineffective. And as long as you remain in denial, the longer you will avoid making the tough decisions about your top priorities.

8. To effectively deal with work overload, people choose the only one way that doesn't work.

So, here are the six ways to deal with too much to do. The first five are effective. Unfortunately, most people go for the sixth.

1. **Accomplish more** - This option is simply wishful thinking unless you actually find a new, faster method that makes a measurable difference. You won't save significant time just trying to be faster and more disciplined.
2. **Postpone** - Some things can wait. Push them out.

3. **Cut corners** - Cutting corners sounds bad, but it isn't. Not everything has to be awesome or perfect. As a recovering perfectionist and software engineer, I know of what I speak! Just because engineers can create products with awesome features, doesn't mean the customer appreciates those features enough to foot the bill! Before starting any task, always ask the question, "How well?" Those last tweaks are usually discernible to no one but yourself.
4. **Ignore** - Some tasks just don't need to be done. Our lists fill up with them thanks to forces such as: consistency for the sake of consistency, old habits, business-as-usual, compulsiveness, favorite activities, bad processes, and unlimited cool ideas.
5. **Delegate or outsource** - Too many people are doing tasks that should never be on their plates in the first place. If you don't know how to delegate effectively and confidently, you need a dose of process clarity. If you are a control freak or simply unwilling to let go, knock it off!
6. **Neglect to choose one of the above** - This is the only ineffective option and the most common method for dealing with too much to do. You have five good options, but they require a conscious decision. What happens when you take option #6? Some tasks are abandoned, others are postposed, and corners are cut. But not by conscious decision.

When we fail to manage ourself, establish top priorities, and make conscious decisions about what to do and what not to do, the stress is unbelievable and the results aren't pretty.

It's time to bite the bullet, narrow your top priorities list to 2 - 3 items at any one time, schedule time on your calendar to tackle those items, and devote the rest of your energy to focusing and getting them done. Quit wasting so much time and energy listing, managing, and prioritizing the things that deserve to fall through the cracks.

Be the Boss of your Time & Life – Take Control

A horse suddenly came galloping quickly down the road. It seemed as though the man had somewhere important to go.

Another man, who was standing alongside the road, shouted, "Where are you going?" and the man on the horse replied,

"I don't know! Ask the horse!"

Time Management at the time of Crisis – Pandemic, Disaster, War

During the pandemic situation like COVID-19 outbreak, many companies are suggesting—even requiring—that more employees work from home. Working from home can be a lonely enterprise in this era of social distancing, but it doesn't have to be. For those who are not used to working at home or who don't have an organized work station, distractions can disrupt your productivity. After all, you're in your personal space, not your usual professional environment. Laundry needs to be done, dishes washed and the house cleaned. Plus, maybe you want to see The View since you're always at the office when it's on, or there's a good movie on Netflix you've been longing to watch. And your spouse keeps yelling questions from another room, causing you to keep loosing your train of thought. Or on the flip side, maybe since being at home 24/7, you find yourself toiling overtime on the job long after you usually would have called it quits at the office. On top of it all, cabin fever could be sneaking up on you.

Productivity Tips For Working From Home

If you're not used to working from home, it can take some getting used to new challenges that you might not have at the office. It's important to have a defined schedule and stick to it. Avoid sleeping in or lingering over breakfast, and get to work just as if you're driving across town to your office, although you might be walking into the next room.

You might think blasting Lady Gaga's latest hit is the most productive way for you to work. Or loud noises could be the worst thing for you to stay focused and get work done. Everybody is different. Some people work better in clutter while others can't concentrate unless their work space is tidy. Regardless of your personal style, here are some tips to facilitate adjusting to your new situation during the Corona virus outbreak:

1. Confine your work space to a specific area in your home so your job doesn't intrude into the lives of other household members and you can concentrate. Have a space that you designate as your workstation instead of checking emails, voicemails or texting in front of TV or spreading work out on the kitchen table. Make your space a stress-free zone of quiet and solitude where you can concentrate. If you don't have a separate room, find an area with minimum traffic flow or a corner of a room off from the main area.
2. Block the neighbor's barking mutt, excess noise from household members or ambient traffic with noise cancelling head phones or ear buds. Studies show that a delicate blend of soft music combined with soothing nature sounds—such as waterfalls, raindrops, a rushing brook or ocean waves—activates the calming part of your brain, helps you concentrate and lowers heart rate and blood pressure.
3. Go to the same designated place on a regular basis so your mind doesn't wander, and you can focus and increase your productivity. Establish water-tight psychological boundaries so you're not constantly reminded of temptations around you (there's chocolate cake in the fridge) or unfinished personal tasks—such as doing laundry, vacuuming or organizing your spice rack—that otherwise could compromise your productivity. And complete these personal activities outside of work hours as you normally would.
4. Set water-tight physical boundaries around your designated work space that is off limits for housemates. Treat it as if it's five miles across town, and ask house members to consider it as such (e.g. no interruptions from another room when you're engrossed in a project unless an emergency). If possible, only go to your designated space when you need to work. Stick to a regular schedule, and keep your work space at arm's-length after hours. Try to maintain the same hours you log in at the office so you don't get swallowed up by the workload.
5. After a reasonable day's work, put away your electronic devices and work tools just as you would store carpentry

tools after building shelves or baking ingredients after making a cake. Keeping work reminders out of sight keeps them out of mind and helps you relax and recharge your batteries.

6. Discourage personal intrusions. If you're a teacher or doctor, friends don't just stop by the office to chat, hangout or interrupt your work. But sometimes well-intended friends, family members and neighbors think working at home is different. Interruptions and drop-ins can cause you to lose your focus, procrastinate or get behind on a deadline. It's important to prevent intrusions into your work space by informing others that although the location of your job has changed, it is no different from any other profession requiring privacy and concentration. Notify others that during at-home work hours you're unavailable and cannot be interrupted. And let them know the after hours when you're available to connect.

7. Employ your video communications perhaps more than you normally would, now that you're more isolated. Make sure you have your company's telecommuting devices—such as Zoom—hooked up and ready to go so you can stay connected with team members or office mates and you're available for video calls and teleconferencing. If you start to feel lonely, consider setting up a support group of friends and colleagues who are also working at home by satellite. Make plans to meet on a regular basis and share creative ways you've adjusted to the new situation.

8. Avoid cabin fever. Now that you're spending a disproportionate amount of time at home, get outside as much as possible with gardening or walking around the block. Mounting research shows that spending time in nature lowers stress, helps you relax and clears your mind. After work hours, enjoy other areas of your home: watching a good movie, reading a book, or cooking a fun meal. And lead as much of a full social life as possible such as having non-symptomatic friends over for dinner. The new normal is not to limit social devices but to take advantage of them. Use Facetime, Facebook or Skype with friends and family

members so you feel connected to the people in your life that you care about.

9. Keep your attitude in check. Above all, be creative and don't let your confined circumstances dwarf your tranquility, happiness or productivity. Your greatest power is your perspective. It can victimize you or empower you. When you look for the upside in a downside situation and figure out what you can control and what you can't, it's easier to accept whatever is beyond your control. Your best ally is to find the opportunity in the difficulty during an uncontrollable situation instead of the difficulty in the opportunity. Take advantage of this restrictive time to clear clutter out of your basement, pull weeds in the garden or get caught up on fun hobbies you've neglected for a while.

"You'll often find that it's not mom or dad, husband or wife, or the kids that's stopping you.
It's you. Get out of your own way."

— **Robert Kiyosaki**

"Purpose of life should be happiness and peaceful life, which spreads wave of making the world better, not bitter.

Plan time-slots for your big issues before anything else, or the inevitable issues will fill up your days and you won't find time to handle the big issues."

— **Richard Feynman**

Time is NOT Money - Time is Our LIFE (Don't trade one for the other)

We all have heard the famous adage "Time is money". To be honest, I don't agree to it. While money is important — I think time is way more important and precious than money. Because time is what our lives are made of. And too many people are trading it for money.

Here's the thing: a person can make more money. There are hundreds of ways we know how to make money. I can teach anyone more ways to do it. But I can't teach anyone how to get back one second of their lives that they have wasted, or traded away to some company in exchange for a paycheck. That time is gone forever.

The "time = money" equation is for employees...

- ➤ They work for an hour, and get paid so much in return
- ➤ Every moment they're not working, they're not getting paid
- ➤ They're trading a non-renewable resource

But when a person has their own business, the equation is turned upside down in a miraculous way. The business makes money, which gives the business owner more time!

Important is how much are you willing to invest in free time

We all know Maslow's Hierarchy of Needs.

According to Maslow, all human beings start with the basic physiological needs—that is needs to survive, such as food, water, clothing, and shelter. From there, things ladder up to safety, love and belonging, esteem, and finally, self-actualization.

For Maslow, self-actualization was becoming the best of your potential, to be what you could be. Many of us long for those, though few achieve it. And you could argue that those who reach the level of self-actualization are constantly creating new areas of achievement.

The fact is that the most successful people in the world are those who excel at living at the level of self-actualization. But there is a key to achieving this level of need that may not be readily apparent—it is, literally, making time.

Making time to succeed

If you've ever had the nagging feeling that you weren't living up to your full potential, you've felt the tug of self-actualization. For most people, that's where it stops, at the tug. After all, we're all very good at making excuses as to why something we long to accomplish is impractical or impossible to accomplish. Sure, it sounds nice in theory, but who's got the time?

If you think about it, if there's one thing extremely successful people seem to have, it's lots of time. You may have asked this at one time, "How do they get so much done?" It seems like successful people have an unnatural ability to do more than the average person.

You may be tempted to think this is because of a harder work ethic, or because they put in the hours. And while that can be true for a few, the reality is that most successful people understand the value of time—and of creating by delegating tasks that suck time up.

Be careful on waste of money

Many of people find problem in outsourcing or hiring people to help him do menial tasks. They forget that **their most important asset is time.**

> "The difference between a poor person and a rich person is how they use their time—and what they're willing to pay for when it comes to time."

A person who value his time doesn't hesitate in paying people to do time-consuming tasks for him, and in return, have unlimited time to accomplish great things. He understand that his time was valuable and that a small investment in a house cleaner and cook afforded him the opportunity to do high-value tasks with his time that only he could do. This is, of course, the principle upon which every successful business is built: hire employees to do specialized tasks so that the business owner can focus his or her time on building and growing the business. Many rich people are rich because they understand this concept and apply it both to business and to life.

Buying time = buying happiness

And there is another upside to this approach to life: happiness. It's often said that money can't buy you happiness, and while that may be true, what money can buy you can make you happy.

Many people have no problem saving "for vacations, personal experiences, going out for nice meals, and health care," but don't seem to feel free to save up and pay for services that would free up time.

In an experiment conducted, after receiving INR 5000 to spend over a weekend on either a material item like a bottle of wine or on time-saving purchases, "people reported that spending money on time-saving purchases left them in a better mood than spending money on material goods."

And when you're in a better mood, you're more pre-disposed to do your best work on things you care about—like build that side business. Ideas flow, productivity increases, and barriers are broken.

It's time to take back your time

If you continue to fight that nagging feeling that you could be doing more, don't push it away. Instead, I encourage you to take a look at how you can invest in creating more time to focus on the passions and goals you have for yourself. Rather than look at a housekeeper as an expense, view it as an investment so that you can achieve your goals and dreams. The key, of course, is to use your free time to do something constructive that moves you toward self-actualization, not just sit on the couch and binge-watch Netflix.

Today, start thinking like the rich when it comes to your time… and just maybe you'll be rich in no time.

Watch yourself

There was once a pair of acrobats. The teacher was a poor widower and the student was a young girl by the name of Radhika. These acrobats performed each day on the streets in order to earn enough to eat.

Their act consisted of the teacher balancing a tall bamboo pole on his head while the little girl climbed slowly to the top. Once to the top, she remained there while the teacher walked along the ground.

Both performers had to maintain complete focus and balance in order to prevent any injury from occurring and to complete the performance. One day, the teacher said to the pupil:

'Listen Radhika, I will watch you and you watch me, so that we can help each other maintain concentration and balance and prevent an accident. Then we'll surely earn enough to eat.'

But the little girl was wise, she answered, 'Dear master, I think it would be better for each of us to watch ourself. To look after oneself means to look after both of us. That way I am sure we will avoid any accidents and earn enough to eat.'

www.ingramcontent.com/pod-product-compliance
Lightning Source LLC
Chambersburg PA
CBHW062207080426
42734CB00010B/1824